JAPANESE SOUPS

66 Nourishing Broths, Stews and Hotpots

KEIKO IWASAKI

TUTTLE Publishing

Tokyo | Rutland, Vermont | Singapore

Contents

Why Japanese Soups?

Delicious and nourishing Japanese-style soups appear on my dining table regularly. Every soup is prepared using a homemade stock, called *dashi* in Japanese. The specific components in each of the different dashi variations create a base flavor that best complements the ingredients.

Soup is a frequent go-to dish in our home, sometimes served as a hearty one-pot meal and at other times enjoyed as a light supper after having a few drinks. Soups offer flexibility that many other dishes do not, as they are quick to put together and easy to digest. They also warm up the body and the soul, supporting overall vitality and health.

The numerous easy-to-make soups in this book are my favorites to prepare and serve in my home.

– Keiko Iwasaki

The Basics

The **5** Benefits of Japanese Soups

1 Gentle on the Body

The Japanese-style soups in this book are based on stocks, called *dashi*, made with various ingredients, including kombu seaweed, bonito flakes (called *katsuobushi* in Japanese) or other dried seafood, as well as flavorful vegetables like shiitake mushrooms. Unlike store-bought broth mixes, a stock prepared from scratch is truly natural and additive-free.

A good stock is the key to a delicious soup that is mild yet satisfying. As long as the stock is rich in umami ("savory deliciousness"), you can go easy on the salt without compromising the flavor. In other words, Japanese-style soups are perfect for those who are watching their sodium intake and looking for ways to address or prevent symptoms of lifestyle diseases.

The soups in this book contain a variety of vegetables which are combined with seafood and meat to maximize the nutritional balance. The easy-to-digest soups are low in calories, making them a perfect choice for a late-night meal.

2 Simple to Make and Delicious

Because the Japanese-style soups in this book are made with umami-rich stock, you don't have to do a great deal to develop the flavors. Simply combine the ingredients with the stock, cook lightly and add the suggested seasonings. In other words, all the recipes you'll find on these pages are very easy to prepare.

Unlike Western-style soups, which are often simmered for a long time over low heat, Japanese soups are energy-efficient and environmentally friendly because they can usually be put together very quickly.

Quick-cooking soups are very convenient, especially when you're busy, or coming home from work late in the evening after a hard day's work. Having a bowl of warm soup is a wonderful way to soothe ruffled edges after a hectic day or hit the spot when you're feeling peckish.

3 Can Be Made Using Simple Ingredients

One of the best things about Japanese-style soups is that you can utilize vegetables, seafood and meat that are readily available at your neighborhood market. Seasonal vegetables tend to have more flavor, so I highly recommend keeping an eye out for what's being harvested near you.

Because they're so flexible, these soups are perfect for when you haven't had the time to go shopping or you have limited ingredients on hand. Once you've built up a stash of Japanese soup staples in your pantry, you'll be able to put together a simple Japanese-style soup whenever the mood takes you.

For example, all you need to make a simple stock is a small quantity of bonito flakes or a few dried shiitake mushrooms. Shio kombu or umeboshi salt-pickled plums can be incorporated as the backbone of the soup. Canned fish, dried daikon radishes and dried seaweed like wakame are also handy options to have around when preparing a Japanese-style soup.

4 Perfect for Weight Management

Because all the soups in this book are nutritionally balanced and low in calories, they are an excellent go-to for those trying to lose weight. The key to keeping the calorie count down is to use as little sugar and oil as possible, avoid roux made with butter and flour and incorporate as many vegetables as you can. If meat is added, you should use lean cuts whenever possible.

While some recipes in this book call for sautéing the vegetables in a small amount of oil to maximize the flavor from the beginning, most of them cook the ingredients in the dashi stock directly. Milk, butter, cheese and other dairy products are used in small amounts to add richness and depth of flavor.

Adding plenty of vegetables ensures that you are getting enough of the vitamins, minerals and dietary fiber that constitute a balanced diet to assist healthy weight loss. Adding seafood to a soup makes it a good source of calcium, which tends to be deficient in many diets.

5 The Soothing Properties of Soup

Japanese-style soups have a rounded flavor that brings comfort and ease with every spoonful. Eating hot soup slowly warms your body from the inside, improving circulation and relaxing your mind.

A hearty stock base also plays a key role in a soothing soup. It is believed that the smell of the broth can work like aromatherapy, loosening you up and helping you unwind.

The ingredients in soup are not hard to chew, which also helps to put you at ease. No need to tackle with a knife and fork, just take a spoonful and let the warm, savory, tender components release your inner tensions.

The 4 Basic Rules for Making Perfect Soups

Rule 1

CREATE UMAMI USING DASHI STOCK
Use dashi made with seafood, meat or vegetables

Rule 2

CREATE FLAVOR USING SEASONINGS
Add soy sauce, salt or miso to the dashi

Rule 3

CREATE DEPTH USING AROMATICS
Step up the flavor with aromatic vegetables,
condiments and spices

Rule 4

IMPROVE THE TASTE WITH INGREDIENT PAIRINGS
Combine ingredients based on robust vs. mild,
heavy vs. light or multiple contrasts

Rule

1

Create Umami Using Dashi Stock

Most of the dashi stocks in this book are made from bonito flakes or other dried seafood, kombu seaweed and other vegetables, or meat. Some recipes use dashi prepared in advance, others incorporate the dashi ingredients into the soup directly. Other recipes extract flavor from the ingredients added (e.g., meat). If a recipe calls for "dashi" without specifying what kind, use any of the ones on the following pages.

Umami sources can be largely classified into three groups: amino acids, nucleic acids and organic acids. Using a single ingredient from one group can boost umami; however, combining ingredients from different groups is highly recommended, as it adds a layer of depth to the flavor. One example is using kombu (from the amino acid group) and bonito flakes (from the nucleic acid group) together.

Three types of dashi stock

 **Seafood dashi**

 **Meat dashi**

 **Vegetable & seaweed dashi**

Seafood Dashi Stock

Seafood has built-in flavor enhancers, including nucleic acids such as inosinates (found in bonito flakes, dried sardines and blue-skinned fish), amino acids such as taurine (found in squid and octopus) and glycine (found in shrimp and crab), and organic acid compounds such as succinic acid (found in shellfish).

Fresh whole fish
Flavor is extracted from the meat and bones of fish like horse mackerel and Pacific sea bream.

Small dried fish
Dried sardines are often used.

Bonito flakes
Often used in combination with kombu.

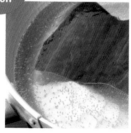

Dried ingredients
Dehydrating concentrates the umami in ingredients such as sakura shrimp.

Fish fillets
Use skin-on fillets of cod and other fish, as the skin also imparts umami.

Shellfish
Scallops and Manila clams, which are used whole, are popular.

Used most often

HOW TO MAKE BONITO DASHI STOCK

❶ Steep the kombu in water

Combine 2½ cups (625 ml) water and a 3-inch (7.5 cm) piece of kombu in a pot. Let the kombu steep for 30 minutes.

Place the pot over medium heat. Remove the kombu when you start seeing small whitish bubbles on its surface.

❷ Add dried bonito flakes

Turn the heat to high and add the bonito flakes.

Remove the pot from the heat when the water comes to a boil.

❸ Strain

Pour the liquid through a fine-mesh strainer lined with cheesecloth or a paper coffee filter.

Meat Dashi Stock

Chicken, pork and ham, which are rich in nucleic acid inosinates, add savor and richness to the stock. Meat in general is a good source of succinic acid, an organic acid compound that enhances flavor.

Ground meat
Umami can be extracted in a short time, as the meat is already in small pieces.

Thinly sliced meat
Short on time? Use thinner slices of meat for optimal flavor.

Bone-in meat
The bones contribute additional flavor to create a savory, high-quality dashi.

Processed meat
The seasonings in bacon and sausage make for a quick and flavorful stock.

Rich and robust

HOW TO MAKE CHICKEN DASHI STOCK

❶ Sear the chicken

Heat oil in a pot as directed in the recipe. Add the quantity of chicken specified.

Sear the meat on both sides to brown and develop flavor.

❷ Add the water

Add the amount of water called for and turn the heat to high. Bring the liquid to a boil and then turn heat to low.

❸ Use the meat as a component of the soup

Simmer for 15 to 20 minutes to let the flavor develop.

Add the remaining ingredients and seasonings to finish the soup.

Vegetable & Seaweed Dashi Stock

The flavor enhancers in vegetables and seaweed include amino acid compounds such as glutamates (found in kombu seaweed, soybeans, sesame seeds and tomatoes) and nucleic acid compounds such as guanylates (found in shiitake and other mushrooms).

Onion
The sweetness and flavor of onion permeate the soup as it cooks.

Kombu Seaweed
Dried kombu or shio kombu add flavor.

Mushrooms
Shiitake and other mushrooms are packed with umami.

Squash
The sweetness of kabocha or butternut squash comes through as umami.

Beans
As well as whole beans, bean products like tofu and soy milk can be used.

Tomato
Tomatoes have the highest level of umami of any vegetable.

Umami-rich

HOW TO MAKE KOMBU DASHI STOCK

① Steep the kombu

Combine 2½ cups (625 ml) water and a 3-inch (7.5 cm) piece of kombu in a pot. Allow to steep for 30 minutes.

② Heat the water

Place the pot over medium heat and bring to a simmer. Small whitish bubbles will form on the surface of the kombu.

③ Remove the kombu

Turn off the heat and promptly remove the kombu before it can become slimy.

Combining Several Dashi Stocks Improves the Flavor

Umami, the "fifth taste," is the savory, moreish quality often highlighted in Japanese food. You can combine different kinds of dashi to multiply umami sources, amplifying the flavor of the soup. This is a great way to expand the range of soups in your repertoire.

When dashi is prepared using kombu and bonito flakes together (page 13), the glutamate from the kombu and the inosinate from the bonito flakes work together to boost the umami in the dashi synergistically.

Some studies show that combining guanylate—found in abundance in shiitake and other mushrooms—with glutamate will multiply umami significantly. Shiitake mushrooms are also a great flavor enhancer in their dried form, and I highly recommend keeping them in your pantry. Reconstitute them in a small amount of water (enough to cover) to maximize the extraction of the umami components.

Using your savvy about flavor enhancers to extract or combine them in the right way will yield great-tasting soups.

Double Dashi Stock

Horse mackerel with bones is a good source of inosinate, a nucleic acid. Combining it with kombu, which is rich in the amino acid glutamate, makes a delectable dashi.

Super umami!

HOW TO MAKE KOMBU AND HORSE MACKEREL DASHI STOCK

❶ Remove fishy odors with boiling water

Remove and discard the head and innards of a whole horse mackerel. Rinse the fish and chop it into chunks.

Lay the pieces in a sieve and pour boiling water over them to remove odor.

❷ Cook the horse mackerel and kombu

Place the fish pieces in a pot and add 2 cups (500 ml) water. Bring to a simmer over medium high heat.

Just before the water starts to boil, remove the kombu.

❸ Continue to cook the horse mackerel

Simmer for 10 minutes.

After five minutes, skim off any foam that rises to the top.

Create Flavor Using Seasonings

The main seasonings used in this book are soy sauce, salt and miso. These are the foundations of classic Japanese-style soups.

Both soy sauce and miso contain a perfect blend of umami components from amino acids, so they add depth to dashi stock when used as seasonings. Salt enhances taste as well, but it is important to avoid refined salt, which has a harsh taste. Natural, unrefined salt has a hint of sweetness and a more subtle taste, and is rich in minerals.

No matter what seasoning you use, it is important not to use too much. Its effect should be mild, not overpowering.

Three types of seasonings

Soy sauce **Salt** **Miso**

Seasoning with Soy Sauce

To make the most of its distinctive savor and aroma, soy sauce should be added toward the end of cooking whenever possible.

Clear Dashi Broth with Soy Sauce

Basic proportions for two servings:
**1 teaspoon of soy sauce for
1¾ cups (425 ml) dashi stock**

╋ Add the dashi stock

All kinds of dashi, including bonito, kombu and seafood-based dashi, work well.

╋ Add the other ingredients

Since soy sauce has a nice aroma, it is wonderful paired with aromatics such as mitsuba (wild Japanese parsley) or green onions.

Seasoning with Salt

When using ingredients such as clams, sea bream and other kinds of fish with full-flavored meat, it is important to use only salt to season the soup. This allows the natural umami of the seafood to shine.

Seafood-based Clear Broth with Salt

Basic proportions for two servings:
**Use ⅓ teaspoon salt for
1¾ cups (425 ml) of dashi stock**

Salt

+ Add the dashi stock

A light dashi made from kombu and/or seafood works well.

+ Add the seafood

Since the broth itself is kept simple, it is best to use umami-rich ingredients.

Seasoning with Miso

The flavor of miso is perfect for seasoning meat and seafood soups that are richer and have more fat. Take care not to boil miso or cook it for too long, as this will diminish the flavor.

Miso Soup

Basic proportions for two servings:
**Use 1 tablespoon of miso for
1¾ cups (425 ml) of dashi stock**

➕ **Add the dashi stock**

Umami-rich dashi, such as one made from dried sardines, bonito flakes or meat, works well.

➕ **Add the other ingredients**

Anything works!

Create Depth Using Aromatics

To make soups more flavorful, I recommend incorporating aromatic vegetables and seasonings. You can also add spices to boost flavor and aroma. Used in combination, aromatic vegetables and pungent spices make the flavor more complex and bring depth to the soup.

Some aromatic vegetables are available in dried or powdered form. Use fresh aromatics, if available, for the best flavor.

Just swapping the aromatics in the recipe can change the flavor significantly. Trying out variations will help to expand the range of your culinary offerings.

Three types of aromatics

Aromatic vegetables	Aromatic condiments	Aromatic herbs & spices
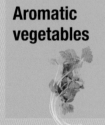		

Aromatic vegetables

Ginger and garlic are added early so their flavor infuses the soup. Mitsuba (wild Japanese parsley) and ginger bud (myoga) should be added toward the end of the cooking process to preserve their freshness.

Garlic   Ginger   Mitsuba   Myoga ginger bud

Aromatic condiments

These ingredients all add aroma and richness to the soup, and sometimes add a colorful touch also. Grated cheese and ground sesame seeds will maximize the aromatic effect.

Ground sesame seeds   Saffron   Sansho pepper   Grated cheese

Aromatic herbs & spices

Depending on how they are used, spices can transform Japanese-style soups in many ways, adding a unique, exotic twist. In addition to providing a touch of heat, spices can bring rich aromas to the table.

Curry powder   Yuzu kosho paste   Ground black pepper   Chili pepper, shichimi pepper blend

Improve the Taste with Ingredient Pairings

Because the soups in this book are seasoned with a light hand, it is important to combine ingredients effectively.

For example, the fat from meat and seafood lends strong umami and deep flavor that is balanced by light-flavored vegetables. If there is a key ingredient whose flavor profile you want to highlight, combine it with a mild-tasting element. If you want to make a hearty soup, limit the number of ingredients to around five items so each flavor comes through.

Sweet vegetables like kabocha or butternut squash are best combined with those that are not so sweet, like eggplant.

Three ingredient pairings

Combine robust + mild flavors	Use light vegetables with meat or fish	Use up to 5 different ingredients

Combine robust + mild flavors

It is important to balance flavor intensity by combining flavor-packed ingredients like sea bream with something more neutral, like baby turnips. The ingredient with the leading flavor is the one that will unify the entire soup.

Sea Bream Soup with Turnips

RECIPE
PAGE
41

Use light vegetables with meat or fish

While the fattiness of meat and fish imparts richness and aroma, it can be overpowering in soups. Adding mild-flavored vegetables helps to create balance so you can savor the soup until the very end.

Sparerib Soup with Lotus Root

RECIPE
PAGE
46

Use up to 5 different ingredients

When combining a variety of ingredients in a soup, try to incorporate contrasting flavor profiles and textures. A sample combination might be a protein, a root vegetable, a strong-tasting vegetable, a mild vegetable and a soybean product.

Chicken and Vegetable Soup

RECIPE
PAGE
62

Glossary of Japanese Ingredients

Aonori Flakes of green nori seaweed. Available at Asian grocery stores. Dulse flakes, sold at natural food stores, can be used as a substitute.

Bamboo shoots Found fresh, vacuum packed or in cans at Asian grocery stores. The canned variety is also available in many regular supermarkets. Most packaged and canned bamboo shoots are pre-boiled. Vacuum-packed bamboo shoots may have particles of harmless white grit in the folds when you cut into the shoot. A quick rinse will remove them. Leftover shoots should be refrigerated in a container with fresh water and used within a few days.

Bitter gourd Known as *goya* in Japan, this green gourd has rough, jagged spikes on the rind. The seeds and white pith should be removed, as they are very bitter. Available at Asian grocery stores, especially Indian markets. Winter melon can be substituted.

Bonito Flakes Also known as *katsuobushi* or *hanakatsuo*, umami-packed bonito flakes are used extensively in Japanese cuisine. They can be found at Asian grocery stores and online in two forms: small packets containing fine shavings that are perfect for toppings, or a large bag containing thicker flakes that are used to make stock.

Burdock root Called *gobo* in Japanese, this long, brown-skinned root vegetable has an earthy aroma and is commonly used in stir fries and soups in Japanese cooking. Scrub with a vegetable brush or gently scrape with the back of a knife instead of peeling the skin. Available at Asian grocery stores. If you can't get hold of it, carrot has a similar texture.

Chrysanthemum greens These greens, called *shungiku* in Japanese, have a distinct flavor. If you can't find them, mustard greens or spinach can be substituted. Available at Asian grocery stores.

Daikon radish A long, white variety of winter radish that is often pickled, eaten raw or simmered in Japanese cuisine. Found in grocery stores in any area with a good-sized Asian population. White radishes or turnips work as substitutes.

Deep-fried tofu skins These pouches are called *abura-age* in Japanese. Often simmered or stuffed, deep-fried tofu skins are also used in miso soup. Available at Asian grocery stores in the refrigerated or frozen section.

Dried sardines Called *niboshi* in Japanese. Many varieties of sun-dried sardines are used in Japanese cooking. Larger ones are used to prepare stock, while smaller baby varieties are eaten as a snack. Available at Asian grocery stores.

Enoki mushrooms A type of mushroom with long stems and small white caps. Available at natural food stores or Asian grocery stores. Oyster mushrooms or white button mushrooms can be substituted.

Garlic chives Known as *nira* in Japanese, this variety of chives imparts a delicate garlic flavor and is often used in dumplings. Available at Asian grocery stores. Green onions or chives make good substitutes.

Glass noodles Also called Chinese vermicelli, cellophane noodles or bean thread noodles, these transparent strands are made from mung-bean starch and water. They are widely used in Asia in stir-fries, soups and spring rolls. Available at Asian grocery stores and online. If they are unavailable, substitute thin rice noodles or angel-hair pasta.

Kabocha squash A type of winter squash with green skin and orange flesh. The skin is edible and does not need to be peeled. Available at natural food stores and Asian grocery stores. Butternut squash or buttercup squash can be used as a substitute.

Komatsuna greens Large leafy green vegetable with a mild, mustard-like flavor. Available at Japanese grocery stores. Substitute mustard greens, bok choy or spinach if komatsuna is not available.

Kombu seaweed A variety of dried kelp commonly used to make stock. Wipe the surface with a damp paper towel before using since rinsing removes the umami flavor. Available at natural food stores, Asian grocery stores or online.

Kombu powder Also known as kelp tea, this powder is slightly salty and briny, packed with umami from the sea. Available at Japanese grocery stores. You can also make your own by pulverizing a piece of dried kombu in a spice grinder.

Konnyaku Gelatinous cake with a distinct chewiness made from the bulb of the konjac plant. It is typically gray from the added seaweed powder. Available in the refrigerated section of Asian grocery stores. Unfortunately, there is no good substitute for konnyaku. You can omit it and increase the amount of other ingredients.

Lotus root The root of the aquatic lotus plant is a mainstay of Asian cooking. It adds a sweet flavor and crunchy texture to soups and other savory dishes. May be found at Asian grocery stores fresh, frozen, dried or vacuum packed. Water chestnuts can be used as a substitute.

Manila clams Also known as Japanese littleneck clams or *asari* in Japanese. They must be soaked in salted water before cooking to expel any sand. Sold live or frozen at Asian grocery stores.

Mirin wine Rice wine with a sweet flavor. Some brands may contain salt, in which case the seasonings must be adjusted accordingly. Available at Asian grocery stores or liquor stores. Sweet white wine may be substituted.

Miso paste Fermented bean paste used widely in Japanese cooking. There are many different varieties available, including barley, brown rice and white miso. In general, lighter miso is milder and sweeter, while darker varieties have a more assertive flavor. Unless specified otherwise, the variety called *awase miso* will probably work best for most of the recipes in this book. It is best to thin the miso with a little bit of liquid before adding to soup to ensure that it dissolves easily. Available at natural food stores and Asian grocery stores. Shelf-stable varieties may be purchased online.

Mitsuba greens Also known as wild Japanese parsley, this spring herb has a refreshingly clean and pleasantly bitter taste. In Japan, it is commonly used in soups, *chawan mushi* (savory egg custard) and *tamagoyaki* omelet. Celery leaves or flat-leaf parsley can be used as a substitute.

Mizuna A variety of Japanese mustard green with a refreshing texture. Can be replaced with arugula or young mustard greens. Available at Asian grocery stores or farmers markets during warmer months.

Myoga ginger bud This rhizome is often added to soups and used as a garnish for chilled tofu and raw fish. Available at Japanese grocery stores. You can use some chopped green onions with grated ginger as a substitute.

Sake lees This byproduct of sake brewing is used to make pickles; it also adds a unique flavor to various dishes. Available at Japanese grocery stores in the refrigerated section or freezer.

Mochi rice cakes Glutinous rice is steamed and then pounded until smooth to create a cake that becomes crispy on the outside and chewy on the inside when toasted. Available at natural food stores, Japanese grocery stores or online in a dried, shelf-stable form.

Nameko mushrooms These small, amber-brown mushrooms have a gelatinous texture. They are often added to miso soup. Available canned or in plastic bags at Asian grocery stores. Some mushroom growers may have them fresh at the farmers' market. If not available, substitute shiitake mushrooms, although the texture is not at all the same.

Sakura shrimp Dried larval shrimp that have a translucent pink color. Despite their small size, they are packed with flavor. Available at Japanese grocery stores or online.

Mochiko rice flour Glutinous rice flour used to make a variety of Japanese sweets. Available at natural food stores, Asian grocery stores or online.

Napa cabbage A long, cylindrical vegetable with tightly packed leaves. Available at Asian grocery stores and natural food stores.

Sansho pepper This relative of Sichuan peppercorn has a citrus flavor and a bit of heat. It is traditionally sprinkled on broiled eel in Japan. Its seeds are also one of the seven main ingredients in *shichimi* pepper blend (see below). Available at Japanese grocery stores or online.

Mountain yam Long, lightskinned tuber with small hair-like roots. The Japanese call it *nagaimo*, and eat it raw or cooked. Wear gloves when handling, as it can irritate the skin. Available at Asian grocery stores. Grated potato or grated taro can be used as a substitute.

Pressed barley Called *oshimugi* in Japan, this flattened type of barley requires less cooking time than the whole (or hulled) variety; it is often cooked together with rice. Available at Asian grocery stores or online. Pearl barley can be used as a substitute.

Shichimi pepper blend A blend of seven spices, this seasoning is often used as a garnish for noodles and soups. Available at Japanese grocery stores or online.

Shio kombu Thin sheets of kombu are boiled in a savory-sweet sauce, then dried and cut into shreds. Called *shio kombu* in Japanese, it makes a wonderful condiment for rice. Sold at Japanese grocery stores or online.

Shirataki noodles Translucent, gelatinous noodles made from konnyaku (see page 27). Sometimes called miracle noodles, they are often sold as a low-calorie alternative for pasta. Available at Asian grocery stores or in the refrigerated tofu section of a regular supermarket. Angel hair or any other thin pasta or noodles can be used as a substitute.

Shiso leaf Sometimes called beefsteak plant, this leafy aromatic green or red herb is a member of the perilla family. Available at Japanese grocery stores. Basil is a fine substitute, especially for recipes containing tomatoes and other summer vegetables.

Shiso pickles These crunchy pickles, called *shibazuke* in Japanese, are made of cucumbers and eggplant with an herbal note from red shiso. Available at Japanese grocery stores or online.

Soba noodles Noodles made of buckwheat flour. Available at natural food stores, Asian grocery stores or online.

Somen noodles These thin noodles made of wheat flour are considered a summer staple in Japan. Available at natural food stores, Asian grocery stores or online.

Taro root A small, round starchy root vegetable with a fibrous husk-like skin. Available at Asian grocery stores.

Tororo kombu Umami-packed thin shavings of dried kombu, also known as *oboro kombu* or shaved kombu. In Japan, tororo kombu is enjoyed on top of rice or in soups (often prepared by simply adding hot water and soy sauce). Buy at Japanese grocery stores or online.

Umeboshi salt-pickled plums Often referred to as a plum in English, this fruit is more closely related to apricots. Umeboshi is a common ingredient in the Japanese diet. Available at Japanese grocery stores or online.

Wakame seaweed A type of sea vegetable that is often added to miso soups and salads. It usually comes prepackaged in dry form. Unless labeled as "cut wakame," which rehydrates instantly, it needs to be reconstituted in a small amount of water before being added to soups. Available at Japanese grocery stores or online.

Winter melon Also known as winter gourd, this large light-green melon has flesh that becomes succulent when simmered. Sold at Asian markets in manageable chunks. Peeled and cored chayote squash makes an acceptable substitute.

Yuzu citrus A tart, very fragrant citrus native to Japan. The zest as well as the juice are used for their aromatic properties. It is available at Asian grocery stores, often in its freeze-dried form. Meyer lemon makes a good substitute.

Yuzu kosho paste This is a condiment made with green chili peppers, yuzu citrus peel and salt. It has a citrusy fragrance and is fairly spicy. Available at Japanese grocery stores or online.

Boosting Richness & Umami

Elevate your soups even more by adding ingredients that will increase the richness and umami toward the end of cooking.

In Japanese cooking, the word *koku*, or richness, is used quite often to refer not only to the intensity of seasoning, but also to the savory flavor that provides satisfaction. It is a term that expresses the depth of flavor in an ingredient or dish.

What kinds of ingredients increase *koku* in Japanese soups?

Dairy products are used to add a creamy texture and mouthfeel. In place of dairy milk, soy milk or sake lees can be added to lend creaminess with a Japanese touch.

To add fragrant aroma and greater complexity to the flavor, use sesame seeds, nuts or kombu-seaweed powder. If you want to add a light, refreshing touch, I highly recommend incorporating canned tomatoes for a perfect balance of acidity and umami.

Ingredients that boost koku and umami

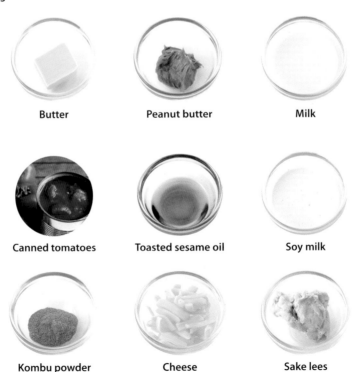

Butter	Peanut butter	Milk
Canned tomatoes	Toasted sesame oil	Soy milk
Kombu powder	Cheese	Sake lees

Fish Soups

Nourishing and Healthy
Fish-Based Soups

In this section, you'll find soups with fish and other seafood that not only add umami to the dashi stock, but also serve as an integral component of the soup.

Slow cooking draws out the flavor into the broth and fills the kitchen with a delightful aroma.

Always add plenty of vegetables for the best balance of flavor and ingredients.

Spicy Scallop Soup

This soup contains scallops and spinach, which are both rich in vitamins and minerals. Scallops are also a good source of taurine, which helps lower cholesterol and prevent high blood pressure.

Serves: 2
Preparation Time: 30 minutes

8 fresh scallops
Salt for sprinkling
½ baby leek or 1 fat green onion
½ bunch spinach
1¾ cups (425 ml) water
1 tablespoon sake
1 teaspoon soy sauce
¼ teaspoon salt
Yuzu kosho paste, to taste, optional

1 Sprinkle the scallops with salt and set aside. Cut the leek or onion in ½-inch (1 cm) pieces and the spinach in 1-inch (2.5 cm) pieces.

2 Combine the water, sake, salted scallops and leek or onion in a pot and bring to a boil over medium-high heat. Reduce heat to low and simmer for 7 to 8 minutes.

3 Add the soy sauce, salt and spinach. When the soup returns to a boil, add the yuzu kosho pepper.

117kcal

| Nourishes the skin | Prevents lifestyle diseases | Anti-aging |

Flavor intensifiers

Scallops and green onions add umami and sweetness. The yuzu kosho paste gives a refreshing, aromatic effect.

Scallops   Green onions   Yuzu kosho paste

Clam Soup with Daikon and Wakame

Mineral-rich Manila clams and wakame seaweed are combined with daikon radish to add a refreshing texture. This gentle, umami-packed soup is good for anemia and hardened arteries.

Serves: 2
Preparation Time: 30 minutes

6–8 Manila clams in shell, soaked
    in salt water to remove sand
2-inch (5 cm) piece daikon
1 teaspoon dried wakame,
    soaked in water to rehydrate
1¾ cups (425 ml) water
1 tablespoon sake
¼ teaspoon salt
Ground sansho pepper, or white
    pepper, to taste

1 Scrub the clams under cold water. Cut the daikon into 1-inch (2.5 cm) lengths, then into matchsticks.

2 Bring the water, sake, daikon and drained clams to a boil in a pot over medium high heat. Reduce heat to low and simmer for 10 minutes. Add the wakame and season with salt.

3 Sprinkle the pepper over before serving.

25kcal

Good for digestion	Wards off lifestyle diseases	Detoxing

Flavor intensifiers

The distinct briny flavor of Manila clams forms the base of this soup. Sprinkling with sansho pepper at the end brings the flavor together.

Manila clams   Sansho pepper

Japanese-style Oyster Chowder

Oysters, which support liver health, are used in this milk-based chowder seasoned with miso. A generous helping of root vegetables supplies vitamins and dietary fiber.

Serves: 2
Preparation Time: 30 minutes

¾ cup shucked oysters, about
    5 oz (150 g)
Salt and pepper for sprinkling,
    plus more for seasoning
1 shiitake mushroom, fresh or
    reconstituted
¼ lotus root (or ½ small can of
    water chestnuts)
2 teaspoons butter
½ carrot, diced
¼ onion, diced
1 cup (250 ml) water
¾ cup (185 ml) milk
½ tablespoon miso, thinned with
    a little of the milk

1 Rinse the oysters and blot dry with paper towels. Sprinkle with salt and pepper. Remove and discard the shiitake mushroom stem and cut the cap into quarters. Peel the lotus root and slice into thin quarter moons.

2 Melt the butter in a pot over medium high heat. Add the carrot, onion and lotus root and sauté. Add the water and shiitake mushroom. Cover and bring to a boil, then reduce heat to low and simmer for 15 minutes.

3 Add the milk and the oysters, and then stir in the miso. Return the soup to a gentle simmer. Adjust the seasoning with additional salt and black pepper.

193kcal | Good for digestion | Nourishes the skin | Anti-aging

Flavor intensifiers

In addition to the flavor extracted from the oysters and shiitake mushroom, miso and butterfat impart richness. Butter and miso go very well together!

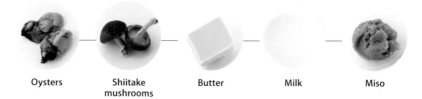

Oysters   Shiitake mushrooms   Butter   Milk   Miso

Egg Flower Soup with Shrimp and Napa Cabbage

Low in fat but high in protein and taurine, shrimp is the perfect food to eat when you are feeling under the weather. Napa cabbage and beaten egg white make the soup soothing and delicious.

97 kcal

Good for digestion | Detoxing

Serves: 2
Preparation Time: 25 minutes

8 raw shrimp
2 leaves napa cabbage
2 teaspoons sake
1¾ cups (425 ml) water
⅓ teaspoon salt
2 teaspoons potato starch or cornstarch
4 teaspoons water
1 egg white, beaten to soft peaks

1 Peel, devein and finely chop the shrimp. Cut the napa cabbage into narrow strips.

2 Combine the napa cabbage, water and sake in a pot. Cover and bring to a boil over medium-high heat. Reduce heat to low and simmer for 10 minutes.

3 Add the shrimp from step 1 and season the broth with the salt. Mix the potato starch with the water and add to the soup. Cook, stirring, until thickened. Turn off the heat and add the beaten egg white to the hot soup, stirring gently to incorporate.

Flavor intensifiers

The sweetness of shrimp melts into the soup. The foamy lightness of the egg white makes this soup fun to eat.

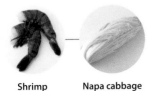

Shrimp   Napa cabbage

Curried Soup with Squid and Mushrooms

Using squid, a low-calorie protein source, this soup is finished with curry powder to add a mellow spiciness. The fiber-rich celery and mushrooms help you feel full without adding many calories.

72kcal

| Good for digestion | Wards off lifestyle diseases |

Serves: 2
Preparation Time: 30 minutes

1 small squid, cleaned, skinned, and sliced into rings
4 oz (100 g) shimeji or other mushrooms
½ stalk celery
1¾ cups (425 ml) water
1 tablespoon sake
2 teaspoons soy sauce
¼ teaspoon curry powder
Salt, to taste

1 Remove the skin from the squid and slice the body into rings. Tear the mushrooms into small clumps. Thinly slice the celery on the diagonal and cut the leaves into bite-sized pieces.

2 Bring the water and sake to a boil in a pot over medium heat. Add the squid, mushrooms and celery and continue cooking until the soup returns to a boil. Season with the soy sauce, curry powder and salt.

Flavor intensifiers

The refreshing aroma of curry powder is accentuated by the flavors of squid, mushrooms and celery.

Squid — Celery — Shimeji mushrooms — Curry powder

Spanish Mackerel and Leek Soup

Packed with health-boosting omega-3 fatty acids and B vitamins, Spanish mackerel plays a starring role in this soup. Searing the fish and the leeks imparts a grilled flavor to the soup and neutralizes any fishiness.

96 kcal

| Nourishes the skin | Boosts metabolism | Wards off lifestyle diseases |

Serves: 2
Preparation Time: 40 minutes

1 fillet Spanish mackerel
Salt for sprinkling, plus ¼ teaspoon for seasoning
1 baby leek or 2 fat green onions
½ red chili pepper
1¾ cups (425 ml) water
2 tablespoons sake
1 teaspoon soy sauce
1 teaspoon rice vinegar
½ teaspoon ginger juice

1 Cut the Spanish mackerel at an angle into 4 pieces and sprinkle with a little salt. Cut the leek or green onions into 1-inch (2.5 cm) pieces.

2 Set a nonstick pan or a cast-iron skillet over medium heat. Place the leek or onions and the mackerel (skin side down) on the hot pan and cook for a couple of minutes until seared. Turn them over and cook the other side.

3 Bring the water and sake to a boil in a pot over medium heat. Add the mackerel, leek or green onions and chili pepper. When the soup returns to a boil, reduce the heat to low and simmer for 7 to 8 minutes. Season with the soy sauce, vinegar, ginger juice and salt.

Flavor intensifiers

The green onions soak up the exquisite stock from the mackerel. The chili pepper adds a nice kick.

Spanish mackerel — Green onions

Crab Soup with Glass Noodles

The orange crab meat and the green leaves make this soup a feast for the eyes as well as for the stomach! Crab meat is high in protein and low in calories. The glass noodles add bulk and a pleasant texture, for a filling and satisfying soup.

75kcal

Nourishes the skin | Wards off lifestyle diseases

Serves: 2
Preparation Time: 30 minutes

¼ cup crab meat, about 2 oz (50 g)
1 stalk chrysanthemum greens, or handful mustard greens
¾ oz (20 g) dry glass noodles or thin rice noodles
1¾ cups (425 ml) dashi stock
1 teaspoon soy sauce
¼ teaspoon salt
2 teaspoons potato starch or cornstarch
4 teaspoons water

1 Pour boiling water over the glass noodles and soak until pliable, then drain and cut into shorter lengths. Cut the greens into 1-inch (2.5 cm) pieces. Break up the crab meat.

2 Bring the dashi to a boil in a pot over medium high heat. Add the glass noodles and crab meat. When the pot returns to a boil, season with the soy sauce and salt. Mix the potato starch with the water and add to the soup, stirring constantly until it thickens.

Flavor intensifiers

You can use inexpensive frozen crab meat in this soup without compromising the flavor. The greens add a refreshing aroma.

Crab — Chrysanthemum greens

Soy Milk Soup with Scallops and Cauliflower

Cauliflower is a good source of potassium, which helps eliminate excess salt. Scallops and soy milk, both rich in protein and low in calories, work in tandem in this soup.

194kcal

| Nourishes the skin | Wards off lifestyle diseases | Anti-aging | Detoxing |

Serves: 2
Preparation Time: 30 minutes

1 baby leek or 2 fat green onions
⅛ head cauliflower
2 teaspoons butter
2 teaspoons all-purpose flour
1 cup (250 ml) water
6 fresh scallops
1 tablespoon sake
¾ cup (185 ml) soy milk
¼ teaspoon salt
Black pepper, to taste
Yuzu citrus or Meyer lemon zest

1 Halve the leek or onions lengthwise and then cut into 1-inch (2.5 cm) pieces. Divide the cauliflower into small florets.

2 Melt the butter in a pot over medium heat. Add the leek or onions and cauliflower florets and sauté. Sprinkle in the flour and brown, stirring to prevent scorching. Add the water, scallops and sake and cover with a lid. Bring to a boil and simmer for 10 minutes, stirring occasionally.

3 Season with the salt and pepper. Add the soy milk and let the pot come back to a boil. Garnish with yuzu or lemon zest.

Flavor intensifiers

The sweet and savory flavors of each ingredient melt into the soy milk to create a perfectly balanced soup.

| Scallops | Green onion | Cauliflower | Soy milk |

Sea Bream Soup with Turnips

Sea bream is rich in umami components such as glutamates and inosinates. The other ingredients are kept simple to highlight the rich seafood flavor.

Serves: 2
Preparation Time: 30 minutes

1 large fillet sea bream
Salt for sprinkling, plus ¼
    teaspoon for seasoning
2 baby turnips, with greens (add
    a handful of mustard greens
    if tops are not available)
1¾ cups (425 ml) dashi stock
1 tablespoon sake

1 Cut the sea bream into bite-sized pieces, sprinkle with salt and let it sit for 10 minutes. Place the pieces in a sieve and pour boiling water over them.

2 Separate the greens from the turnips. Peel and cut the turnips into wedges. Mince the turnip greens.

3 Bring the dashi, turnips and sake to a boil in a pot over medium heat. Add the sea bream, lower the heat and simmer for 10 minutes. Season with the remaining salt, add the turnip greens and simmer for another minute.

80kcal	Good for digestion	Wards off lifestyle diseases	Detoxing

Flavor intensifiers

Rich in umami components, sea bream makes a wonderful broth, even when the bones are not used.

Sea bream

Horse Mackerel Soup with Okra

Chunks of bone-in horse mackerel make a mouthwatering dashi stock. The tanginess of umeboshi salt-pickled plum provides a bright contrast. The omega-3 fatty acids in the fish promote healthy circulation.

69kcal

Good for digestion	Wards off lifestyle diseases

Serves: 2
Preparation Time: 30 minutes

1 whole horse mackerel
Salt for sprinkling, plus ¼ teaspoon for seasoning
4 pods okra
1 myoga ginger bud
1¾ cups (425 ml) water
2-inch (5 cm) piece kombu
1 tablespoon sake
1 umeboshi salt-pickled plum, pitted and halved

1 Scale and clean the horse mackerel and remove the head. Rinse the body very well under running water. Chop the body, bones and all, into 4 pieces and sprinkle with some salt. After 10 minutes, place them in a sieve and pour boiling water over them to remove fishiness.

2 Sprinkle additional salt over the okra, massage by hand and cut each pod in half diagonally. Cut the myoga ginger bud in half lengthwise.

3 Bring the water, kombu, horse mackerel and sake to a boil in a pot over medium heat. Remove the kombu, reduce heat to low and cook for 10 minutes. Add the okra and myoga, season with the salt and let the pot return to a boil. Top each serving with half an umeboshi salt-pickled plum.

Flavor intensifiers

Umeboshi and myoga completely neutralize the fishiness of horse mackerel, leaving only the umami.

Horse mackerel	Myoga ginger bud	Umeboshi salt-pickled plum

Meaty Soups

Meat-Based Soups Boost Stamina and Promote Health

The richness of chicken, pork and beef all impart a profound umami to soups. Don't discard the meat after using it for the basic stock! Keep it as one of the ingredients to really enhance the meaty flavor of the soup.

Meat and Potato Soup

This is a modified version of a popular Japanese meat-and-potato dish called *nikujaga*. Omitting the sugar that is usually added to the traditional version and going light on the seasonings make this hearty soup a very healthy option.

Serves: 2
Preparation Time: 30 minutes

2 potatoes, peeled
2½ oz (60 g) shirataki noodles
¼ onion
3–4 thin slices beef, about 4 oz (100 g)
1 teaspoon vegetable oil
1¾ cups (425 ml) bonito dashi stock (page 13)
1 tablespoon sake
1 tablespoon mirin
1 tablespoon soy sauce
Salt, to taste

1 Cut the potatoes into bite-sized pieces and soak in water. Parboil the shirataki noodles for a few minutes, then drain and cut into shorter strands. Cut the onion into wedges. Cut the beef into bite-size pieces.

2 Heat the oil in a pot over medium heat and sauté the onion. Add the drained potatoes, shirataki noodles and beef. Stir, then add the dashi and sake and cover the pot.

3 When the liquid comes to a boil, reduce the heat to low and simmer for 15 minutes. Add the mirin, soy sauce and salt, simmer a few more minutes, then serve.

244kcal | Good for digestion | Detoxing

Flavor intensifiers

This full-flavored dashi stock adds great depth to the flavor. The vegetables bring a delicious touch of sweetness to the soup.

Beef — Onion — Potato

164kcal | Good for digestion | Wards off lifestyle diseases | Anti-aging

Sparerib Soup with Lotus Root

Simmered well, bone-in pork spareribs lend richness and umami. Lotus root adds crunch, and the greens add an appetizing aroma.

Serves: 2
Preparation Time: 45 minutes

7 oz (200 g) pork spareribs, about 2 inches (5 cm) long
⅔ teaspoon salt, divided
Ground pepper, to taste
½ lotus root (or 1 small can of water chestnuts)
1 stalk chrysanthemum greens, or small handful mustard greens
2 cups (500 ml) water
2 tablespoons sake
½ teaspoon soy sauce
Ground sansho pepper, or ground white pepper, to taste

1 Bring a pot of water to a boil. Add the spareribs and boil for one minute. Rinse under cold running water. Wipe off the moisture with paper towels and sprinkle with half the salt and the pepper. Peel and cut the lotus root into triangular chunks and chop the greens into 1-inch (2.5 cm) pieces.

2 Combine the spareribs, lotus root, water and sake in a pot. Cover and bring to a boil over medium high heat. Reduce heat to low and simmer for 30 minutes.

3 Add the soy sauce, remaining salt and the greens. Cook for a minute or two. Sprinkle with pepper before serving.

Flavor intensifiers

The deep flavor of the bone-in pork is absorbed by the vegetables as they simmer together.

Spareribs   Chrysanthemum greens

Cabbage Soup with Pork Meatballs

The pork flavor is packed into the meatballs, which are cooked together with shredded cabbage and sweet corn. Break up the meatballs to let the flavor seep into the soup.

Serves: 2
Preparation Time: 30 minutes

¾ cup ground pork, about 5 oz (150 g)
½ teaspoon ginger juice
Salt and pepper, to taste
2 tablespoons minced green onion
3 cabbage leaves
1¾ cups (425 ml) water
1 tablespoon sake
5 tablespoons frozen or fresh
    sweet corn
½ tablespoon soy sauce

1 To make the meatballs, combine the ground pork, ginger juice and salt and pepper. Knead by hand until it becomes a thick paste. Add the minced green onion and divide the mixture into fourths. Shape each portion into a ball and then flatten into a disc.

2 Cut the cabbage into thick strips. Bring the water and sake to a boil in a pot and add the meatballs from step 1. Let the pot return to the boil and add the cabbage and sweet corn. Cover and cook for 15 minutes. Before serving, season with the soy sauce and additional salt if needed.

166kcal · Good for digestion · Combats fatigue · Detoxing

Flavor intensifiers

Ground pork imparts richness to the soup. Sweet corn adds sweetness and the green onion has an aromatic effect.

Ground pork   **Sweet corn**   **Green onions**

Spicy Soup with Eggplant and Garlic Chives

Pork and garlic chives provide vitamin B1 to boost stamina. The eggplant soaks up the umami-rich broth for a melt-in-your mouth burst of flavor.

Serves: 2
Preparation Time: 30 minutes

2 slender Asian eggplants
5 stems garlic chives (or green parts of green onions)
½ tablespoon toasted sesame oil
½ cup ground pork, about 4 oz (100 g)
Pinch minced ginger
1¾ cups (425 ml) water
1 tablespoon sake
2 teaspoons soy sauce
Shichimi pepper blend, to taste, optional

1 Remove the eggplant stems. Peel the skin to form a striped pattern, then cut in half lengthwise and slice diagonally. Cut the garlic chives into 1-inch (2.5 cm) pieces.

2 Heat the sesame oil in a pot and sauté the ground pork and minced ginger. Add the eggplant slices and continue to sauté. Add the water and sake, cover and bring to a boil. Lower the heat and simmer for 10 minutes.

3 Stir in the soy sauce, garlic chives and shichimi pepper blend and let the soup return to a gentle simmer.

134kcal · Combats fatigue

Flavor intensifiers

Sautéing the pork and ginger in oil beforehand releases their savor into the soup.

Ground pork — Ginger

Peanut Miso Soup with Pork and Vegetables

The vegetables are flavorful and have plenty of bulk to make you feel full. The richness of peanut butter adds a savory quality and tempting aroma to the soup.

Serves: 2
Preparation Time: 30 minutes

3–4 thin slices pork belly, about
 4 oz (100 g)
½ baby leek or 1 fat green onion
⅓ medium carrot
¼ block konnyaku, about 2½ oz (60 g)
⅓ teaspoon salt
1¾ cups (425 ml) bonito dashi stock
 (page 13)
3 oz (80 g) cauliflower florets
1 tablespoon miso
1 tablespoon unsweetened and
 unsalted peanut butter
Chopped peanuts, for garnish

1 Cut the pork into bite-sized pieces. Cut the leek or green onion into 1-inch (2.5 cm) pieces and the carrot into triangular chunks. Tear the konnyaku into small pieces, sprinkle with the salt and massage briefly, then rinse.

2 Bring the dashi, carrot and konnyaku to a boil in a pot over medium high heat. Add the pork, cover and reduce heat to low. Simmer for 15 minutes, then add the cauliflower and leek or green onion and cook for another 4 to 5 minutes.

3 Mix the miso and peanut butter together and thin with some of the broth from the pot. Stir into the soup and return to a gentle simmer. Garnish with chopped peanuts to serve.

199kcal

Good for digestion	Combats fatigue	Wards off lifestyle diseases	Detoxing

Flavor intensifiers

Combining peanut butter with miso gives a this soup a gentle nuttiness that is irresistible.

Pork   Cauliflower   Carrot   Peanut butter

123kcal | Good for digestion | Detoxing

Pork Belly and Vegetable Soup

Packed with vegetables rich in dietary fiber, this soup is great for keeping in trim while helping you feel full. Cut the pork into thin strips to match the vegetables.

Serves: 2
Preparation Time: 30 minutes

2–3 slices pork belly, about 2 oz (50 g)
Salt, for sprinkling
2-inch (5 cm) piece daikon
3-inch (7.5 cm) piece burdock
1 shiitake mushroom, fresh or reconstituted
2 sprigs flat-leaf parsley
1¼ cups (300 ml) bonito dashi stock (page 13)
1 teaspoon soy sauce
Salt and pepper, to taste

Flavor intensifiers

The flavors of shiitake mushroom, burdock and parsley are delicately balanced in this soup.

1 Cut the pork belly into strips and sprinkle with salt. Cut the daikon and burdock into matchsticks. Soak the burdock in water. Discard the shiitake mushroom stem and slice the cap thinly. Cut the parsley into 1-inch (2.5 cm) pieces.

2 Bring the dashi to a boil in a pot. Add the pork and drained burdock and then return to the boil. Add the daikon and shiitake and cook for a few minutes more, until daikon and burdock are tender.

3 Season with the soy sauce, salt and pepper. Garnish with the parsley.

Pork   Shiitake mushrooms   Burdock   Parsley

Pork and Bitter Gourd Soup

This soup is inspired by the Okinawan stir-fry *chanpuru*. Bitter gourd, rich in vitamin C, is known to lessen fatigue and improve skin condition.

Serves: 2
Preparation Time: 20 minutes

1 small bitter gourd, about 4 oz (100g), or equivalent amount of winter melon
3–4 slices pork loin, about 4 oz (100 g)
Piece firm tofu, about 4 oz (100 g)
1 teaspoon toasted sesame oil
1¾ cups (425 ml) bonito dashi stock (page 13)
1 tablespoon sake
1 teaspoon soy sauce
¼ teaspoon salt
Bonito flakes, for garnish

1 Slice the bitter gourd into ¼-inch (6 mm) thick rings. Use a spoon to scoop out and discard the seeds and pith. Cut the pork loin into bite-sized pieces. Blot the tofu with paper towels to remove excess moisture and cut it into 1-inch (2.5 cm) cubes.

2 Heat the oil in a pot over medium high heat and sauté the pork, bitter gourd and tofu for a few minutes. Add the dashi and sake and bring to a boil.

3 Season with the soy sauce and salt. Sprinkle the bonito flakes over before serving.

| 139kcal | Nourishes the skin | Combats fatigue | Anti-aging |

Flavor intensifiers

The astringency of the bitter gourd is refreshing. The bonito flakes sprinkled on at the end boost flavor.

Pork   Bitter gourd

Chicken Wing and Daikon Radish Soup

The bone-in chicken wings add flavor and collagen to the soup. The mildness of the vegetables acts as an excellent foil for the hearty umami of the wings.

Serves: 2
Preparation Time: 30 minutes

5-inch (13 cm) length daikon radish
¼-inch (6 mm) piece ginger
4 to 5 stalks mizuna greens, or arugula
1 teaspoon vegetable oil
4 chicken wings
2 cups (500 ml) water
1 tablespoon sake
¼ teaspoon salt

1 Peel and cut the daikon radish into cubes. Slice the ginger thinly. Cut the mizuna into 1-inch (2.5 cm) pieces.

2 Heat the vegetable oil in a pot over medium heat. Add the chicken wings and cook until golden brown on both sides. Add the water, sake, daikon and ginger. Cover the pot and let it come to a boil, then reduce the heat to low and simmer for 15 to 20 minutes.

3 Season with the salt; add the mizuna at the end.

128kcal	Good for digestion	Nourishes the skin	Detoxing

Flavor intensifiers

The delicious chicken-based broth is the highlight of this soup. The ginger adds a zippy note.

Chicken wings   Ginger

Chicken and Taro Soup with Yuzu Citrus

The substance that gives taro roots their slippery texture is known to help lower cholesterol and blood pressure and support stomach and liver function. The addition of chicken makes this soup very filling!

Serves: 2
Preparation Time: 30 minutes

1 small chicken breast, about 4 oz
   (100 g)
2 large taro roots
Salt, for sprinkling and seasoning
2-inch (5 cm) piece kombu
1¾ cups (425 ml) water
1 tablespoon sake
½ tablespoon soy sauce
1 slice yuzu citrus or Meyer lemon

1 Cut the chicken breast into bite-sized pieces. Peel the taro roots, cut them into wedges lengthwise and then halve them crosswise. Sprinkle with salt and massage to remove the slippery coating. Rinse under cool water.

2 Combine the water, kombu, sake, taro and chicken in a pot over medium high heat. Remove the kombu when the pot comes to a boil. Reduce heat to low, cover and simmer for 20 minutes.

3 Season with the soy sauce and additional salt to taste. Garnish each serving with half a slice of yuzu.

134kcal

| Good for digestion | Wards off lifestyle diseases |

Flavor intensifiers

The taro roots take on both the fragrance of the yuzu and the hearty savor of the chicken in the broth.

Chicken   Yuzu

| 133kcal | Good for digestion | Nourishes the skin | Wards off lifestyle diseases | Anti-aging | Detoxing |

Chicken and Broccoli Soup with Lotus Root

This well-balanced soup works wonders for the body, inside and out. The lotus root adds textural interest. Potato can be substituted for the lotus root if needed.

Serves: 2
Preparation Time: 30 minutes

1–2 boneless chicken thighs, about 4 oz (100g)
Salt and pepper, to taste
¼ large head broccoli
⅓ medium sized lotus root (or ½ small can of water chestnuts)
1¾ cups (425 ml) water
1 tablespoon sake
⅓ teaspoon salt

1 Cut the chicken thighs into bite-sized pieces and sprinkle with some salt and pepper. Cut the broccoli into small florets. Peel and grate the lotus root on the finest side of a box grater.

2 Combine the water, sake and chicken in a pot over medium high heat. Bring to a boil, then reduce heat to low and simmer for 10 minutes.

3 Add the broccoli, salt and grated lotus root. Return to a boil and cook for 2 to 3 more minutes.

Flavor intensifiers

Salt alone is used to season this soup, enhancing the deep flavor of the chicken-based broth.

Chicken

Tomato Soup with Chicken Meatballs

This tangy and comforting soup features chicken meatballs and antioxidant-rich tomato. Adding soy sauce at the end gives it a Japanese twist.

Serves: 2
Preparation Time: 30 minutes

¾ cup ground chicken, about 5 oz (150 g)
1 tablespoon minced green onion
1 teaspoon plus 1 tablespoon sake, divided
¼ teaspoon salt
2 dashes black pepper, divided
1 large tomato
4 green chives
1¾ cups (425 ml) water
2 teaspoons soy sauce
1 teaspoon grated Parmesan cheese

1 Combine the ground chicken, minced green onion, 1 teaspoon sake, salt, and one dash of the pepper in a bowl. Knead by hand until the mixture becomes a thick paste. Cut the tomato into bite-sized chunks. Cut the chives into 1-inch (2.5 cm) pieces.

2 Bring the water and 1 tablespoon sake to a boil in a pot. Divide the meatball mixture from step 1 into six portions. Shape each portion into a ball and add to the pot. Stir in the tomato and cover. Bring to a boil, then lower the heat and simmer for 10 minutes.

3 Add the soy sauce, remaining black pepper and chives. Sprinkle with Parmesan cheese before serving.

149kcal

Nourishes the skin	Wards off lifestyle diseases	Anti-aging

Flavor intensifiers

The meatballs release flavor into the soup as they are broken apart. The Parmesan cheese deepens the umami.

Ground chicken   Green onions   Tomato   Parmesan cheese

Lemony Soup with Chicken and Winter Melon

The gentle flavor of winter melon provides soothing contrast to the umami from the ground chicken. The heat from the chili pepper boosts the body's metabolism.

Serves: 2
Preparation Time: 30 minutes

10 oz (300 g) winter melon, or
    2 chayote squashes
1 fresh red chili pepper
1 teaspoon toasted sesame oil
½ cup ground chicken, about
    4 oz (100 g)
½ teaspoon ginger juice
1¾ cups (425 ml) water
1 tablespoon sake
⅓ teaspoon salt
Black pepper, to taste
2 teaspoons lemon juice
2 lemon slices, halved crosswise

1 Peel the winter melon, remove the seeds and pulp and cut it into cubes. Cut the chili pepper on the diagonal.

2 Heat the oil in a pot and add, in order, the ground chicken, ginger juice, water, winter melon, sake and chili pepper, stirring between each addition. Cover the pot and bring to a boil. Reduce heat to low and simmer for 15 minutes.

3 Season with the salt, black pepper and lemon juice. Garnish with the lemon slices before serving.

123kcal   Good for digestion   Boosts metabolism

Flavor intensifiers

Ground chicken is magical when it comes to making a rich and savory broth. The tartness of lemon brings the flavors together.

Chicken   Lemon

373kcal

| Good for digestion | Nourishes the skin | Wards off lifestyle diseases |

Miso-tomato Stew with Chicken

Skin-on chicken and vegetables are cut into chunks to make this hearty soup. The combination of tomato purée and miso makes for irresistible flavor.

Serves: 2
Preparation Time: 40 minutes

2–3 boneless chicken thighs, about 8 oz (200 g)
Salt and pepper, to taste
¼ onion
½ medium carrot
1 sweet potato, about 5 oz (150 g)
½ stalk celery
1 tablespoon butter
3 tablespoons red wine
3 tablespoons tomato purée
1¾ cups (425 ml) water
2-inch (5 cm) piece kombu
1 tablespoon red miso

1 Cut the chicken into quarters and season with salt and pepper. Cut the onion into wedges. Cut the carrot and sweet potato into 1½-inch (4 cm) lengths and then quarter them lengthwise. Soak the sweet potato in water. Cut the celery into triangular chunks.

2 Melt the butter in a pot over medium heat and cook the chicken thighs until golden brown on both sides. Add the vegetables, draining the sweet potato first. Sauté for a few minutes and then add the red wine. Stir in the tomato purée, water and kombu. Cover and bring to a boil, then lower heat and simmer for 20 minutes.

3 Remove the kombu. Thin the miso with some of the broth from the pot and stir in. Adjust the seasoning with additional salt and pepper before serving.

Flavor intensifiers

The skin on the chicken yields a lot of flavor, so leave it on unless you are counting calories. The vegetables lend sweetness to the soup.

Chicken

Japanese sweet potato

Onion

Celery

Tomato purée

Chicken and Vegetable Soup

Umami-rich mushrooms and mountain yam, both low in calories and high in fiber, are simmered together with chicken. All the ingredients work together to create a flavorful and deeply satisfying soup.

Serves: 2
Preparation Time: 30 minutes

1–2 boneless chicken thighs, about 4 oz (100 g)
2-inch (5 cm) piece mountain yam
Large handful shimeji or other mushrooms, about 2 oz (50 g)
1 stalk komatsuna greens
1¾ cups (425 ml) water
1 tablespoon sake
½ tablespoon soy sauce
Salt, to taste

1 Cut the chicken into bite-sized pieces. Peel the mountain yam and cut into bars. Remove the base of the mushrooms and pull them apart into smaller clumps. Cut the komatsuna into 1-inch (2.5 cm) pieces.

2 Combine the water, sake, chicken, mountain yam and mushrooms in a covered pot. Bring to a boil over medium heat, then lower the heat and simmer for 10 minutes.

3 Add the komatsuna and allow the soup to return to the boil. Season with the soy sauce and salt.

166kcal

| Good for digestion | Combats fatigue | Wards off lifestyle diseases |

Flavor intensifiers

When cooked, mountain yam becomes pleasantly starchy and creamy, creating an enjoyable textural contrast with the mushrooms.

Chicken

Mountain yam

Shimeji mushrooms

232kcal | Good for digestion | Anti-aging | Detoxing

Chicken and Turnip Soup with Soy Milk

Sake lees help prevent lifestyle diseases and contain fiber and nutrients that support gut health. This creamy soup also contains turnips, which have a detoxifying effect, and soy milk that provides high-quality protein.

Serves: 2
Preparation Time: 30 minutes

4 teaspoons sake lees
1 tablespoon bonito dashi stock
   (page 13)
5 oz (150 g) boneless chicken breasts
2 baby turnips
1 cup (250 ml) water
¾ cup (185 ml) soy milk
¼ teaspoon salt

1 Combine the sake lees with the dashi to soften. Cut the chicken into chunks on the diagonal. Peel the turnips and cut into quarters.

2 Bring the water, chicken and turnips to a boil in a covered pot over medium heat. Reduce heat and simmer for 15 minutes.

3 Mix in the sake lees, soy milk and salt and let the soup return to a gentle boil before serving.

Flavor intensifiers

Chicken, sake lees and soy milk all have abundant umami. The turnips melt in the mouth, promoting a sense of ease.

Chicken   Turnip   Sake lees   Soy milk

Japanese-style Beef Soup

With thick slices of beef, this hearty soup gives you stamina. In addition to adding flavor, burdock and shiitake provide a healthy dose of fiber.

Serves: 2
Preparation Time: 50 minutes

3-4 thick slices beef, about 5 oz (150 g)
Salt and pepper, to taste
3-inch (7.5 cm) piece burdock, or carrot
2 napa cabbage leaves
½ onion
2 shiitake mushrooms, fresh or reconstituted, stems
    discarded
1 baby turnip
½ clove garlic
1¾ cups (425 ml) water
1 tablespoon sake
½ can diced tomatoes
2 teaspoons soy sauce

1 Cut the beef into bite-size pieces and season with salt and pepper. Scrape away the skin of the burdock with the back of a knife. Cut into 2-inch (5 cm) lengths and then cut in half lengthwise. Soak the pieces in water and drain just before using.

2 Cut the napa cabbage into 2-inch (5 cm) pieces. Halve the onion and shiitake mushroom caps. Peel the turnip and cut in half.

3 Combine the beef, vegetables, garlic, water and sake in a covered pot over medium heat. Bring to a boil, then lower the heat and simmer for 30 minutes. Add the tomatoes and cook for 10 more minutes. Season with the soy sauce and additional black pepper.

Flavor intensifiers

The sweetness of the vegetables, the umami from the tomatoes and the richness of the beef all blend together to elevate the flavor of this soup beautifully.

| Beef | Burdock | Napa cabbage | Onion | Shiitake mushrooms | Canned tomatoes |

225kcal | Good for digestion | Nourishes the skin | Wards off lifestyle diseases | Anti-aging | Detoxing

Sesame Miso Soup with Beef and Watercress

A generous helping of nutritious sesame seeds gives this soup wonderful flavor. The bite of the watercress makes for a perfect balance of flavors.

Serves: 2
Preparation Time: 20 minutes

3–4 thin slices beef, about 4 oz
    (100 g)
½ medium carrot
⅓ bunch watercress
1¾ cups (425 ml) bonito dashi stock
    (page 13)
1 tablespoon sake
1 tablespoon miso
2 teaspoons ground sesame seeds
Toasted sesame seeds, for garnish

1 Cut the beef into bite-sized pieces. Slice the carrot into matchsticks and cut the watercress into 1-inch (2.5 cm) pieces.

2 Combine the dashi, sake, beef and carrot in a pot over medium high heat. Cover and bring to a boil, then reduce the heat to low and simmer for 4 to 5 minutes.

3 Thin the miso with some of the soup broth. Stir it into the soup together with the ground sesame seeds and watercress. Cook for another minute or two. Sprinkle with sesame seeds before serving.

157 kcal

Good for digestion	Nourishes the skin	Wards off lifestyle diseases

Flavor intensifiers

This soup showcases the rich flavor and texture of sesame seeds. Bonito dashi stock enhances the umami of the beef.

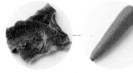

Beef   Carrot   Sesame seeds

Vegetable Soups

Soothe the Palate and the Soul with Vegetable-Based Soups

Umami-rich mushrooms and naturally sweet vegetables and legumes give soups a delicate flavor that soothes the palate and the soul. Vegetables soften and blend perfectly into soups when cooked, creating delicious dishes that are packed with vitamins, minerals, and dietary fiber.

Cabbage, Mushroom and Cherry Tomato Soup

All the vegetables in this soup contribute to a tasty broth. Cherry tomatoes mellow when cooked, lending a savory flavor.

Serves: 2
Preparation Time: 25 minutes

2 napa cabbage leaves
2 shiitake mushrooms, fresh or reconstituted, stems discarded
6 cherry tomatoes
1¾ cups (425 ml) water
1 teaspoon soy sauce
⅓ teaspoon salt
Black pepper, to taste
2 pinches dried sakura shrimp, finely chopped, optional

1 Slice the napa cabbage into ribbons. Cut the shiitake mushroom caps into quarters. Remove the stems of the cherry tomatoes.

2 Combine the water, napa cabbage, shiitake mushrooms and cherry tomatoes in a pot over high heat. Cover and bring to a boil, then reduce heat to low and simmer for 15 minutes.

3 Season with the soy sauce, salt and pepper. Garnish with the chopped sakura shrimp.

41 kcal	Good for digestion	Wards off lifestyle diseases	Detoxing

Flavor intensifiers

The subtle sweetness of the vegetable broth is accentuated by the umami-packed sakura shrimp.

| Napa cabbage | Shiitake mushrooms | Sakura shrimp | Cherry tomatoes |

Mixed-bean Chowder

Beans are a rich source of high-quality protein and fiber that can help mitigate lifestyle diseases. Use precooked mixed beans so that this soup is ready in a snap!

Serves: 2
Preparation Time: 20 minutes

¼ onion
1½ oz (40 g) shimeji mushrooms, or other mushrooms
4 green beans
2 teaspoons butter
⅓ cup cooked mixed beans, drained
1¼ cups (300 ml) bonito dashi stock (page 13)
½ cup (125 ml) milk
1 teaspoon soy sauce
¼ teaspoon salt
Black pepper, to taste

1 Dice the onion. Remove the base of the mushrooms and pull them apart into smaller clumps. Cut the green beans into 1-inch (2.5 cm) pieces.

2 Melt the butter in a pot over medium heat and sauté the onion until soft. Add the mushrooms, green beans and mixed beans and cook for a few more minutes. Stir in the dashi, cover and let the pot come to a boil. Reduce heat to low and simmer for 10 minutes.

3 Stir in the milk. Season with the soy sauce, salt and pepper and return to a gentle simmer.

140kcal

| Good for digestion | Wards off lifestyle diseases |

Flavor intensifiers

Sautéed onion lends sweetness and combines with the milk to make the soup even creamier.

Onion   Shimeji mushrooms   Milk

| 65kcal | Good for digestion | Nourishes the skin | Anti-aging | Detoxing |

Egg-drop Soup with Broccoli and Leek

The sulfur compounds in leeks, the quercetin in broccoli and the fiber in enoki mushrooms work together to support healthy detoxification. A beaten egg is added at the end for greater heft and nutrition, making the soup even more satisfying.

Serves: 2
Preparation Time: 15 minutes

¼ **large head broccoli**
½ **baby leek or 1 fat green onion**
½ **bunch enoki or other**
    mushrooms, ends trimmed
1 **egg, beaten**
1¾ **cups (425 ml) bonito dashi**
    stock (page 13)
1 **teaspoon soy sauce**
⅓ **teaspoon salt**

1 Cut the broccoli into small florets and slice the leek into 1-inch (2.5 cm) pieces. Halve the enoki mushrooms crosswise.

2 Bring the dashi to a boil in a pot. Add the broccoli, leek and enoki mushrooms. Simmer for 2 to 3 minutes over low heat.

3 Season with the soy sauce and salt. Slowly pour the beaten egg into the soup while stirring.

Flavor intensifiers

Thin, delicate strands of enoki mushrooms are packed with flavor. They add bulk to the soup with minimal calories.

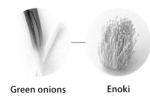

Green onions   Enoki
                    mushrooms

100kcal | **Boosts metabolism** | **Wards off lifestyle diseases** | **Anti-aging** | **Detoxing**

Napa Cabbage and Ham Soup with Ginger

The natural heat of ginger in this comforting soup helps improve circulation and boost metabolism. The ham and the soy milk mellow out the pungency of ginger.

Serves: 2
Preparation Time: 20 minutes

2 napa cabbage leaves
2 slices ham
¼-inch (6 mm) piece ginger
¾ cup (185 ml) kombu dashi
   stock (page 15)
1 cup (250 ml) soy milk
Pinch salt

1 Slice the napa cabbage and the ham into thin strips. Cut the ginger into slivers.

2 Bring the dashi to a boil in a pot over medium heat. Add the napa cabbage, ham and ginger. Cover and simmer for 10 minutes over low heat.

3 Add the soy milk and bring to a gentle boil. Season with the salt.

Flavor intensifiers

Ham, even the inexpensive kind, is an excellent flavor enhancer. Napa cabbage and soy milk add sweetness.

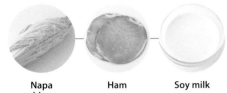

Napa cabbage   Ham   Soy milk

Miso Soup with Daikon and Baby Bok Choy

Asian greens like baby bok choy are a good source of beta-carotene. The shiitake mushroom and dried shredded daikon, both of which are rich in umami, make this soup replete with Japanese flavors.

Serves: 2
Preparation Time: 15 minutes

3½ oz (100 g) dried shredded daikon
1 shiitake mushroom, fresh or reconstituted, stem discarded
½ head baby bok choy
1 tablespoon dried baby sardines
1¾ cups (425 ml) water
1 tablespoon miso

1 Rinse the dried daikon and cut into shorter strands. Thinly slice the shiitake mushroom cap. Cut the baby bok choy diagonally into 1-inch (2.5 cm) pieces.

2 Bring the water, dried baby sardines, dried daikon and shiitake mushroom to a boil in a pot over medium high heat. Reduce heat to low, cover and simmer for 4 to 5 minutes.

3 Add the baby bok choy. Thin the miso with a small amount of broth from the pot, then stir it into the soup and return to a gentle simmer.

39kcal | Good for digestion | Wards off lifestyle diseases | Anti-aging | Detoxing

Flavor intensifiers

Dried vegetables and fish make for a rich broth, as dehydration concentrates flavor.

Dried shredded daikon   Shiitake mushrooms   Dried baby sardines

Egg-topped Cabbage Soup

The sunny-side up fried egg tops a soup of cabbage simmered in dashi stock, upgrading a simple dish into a feast. Cook the egg to your liking.

Serves: 2
Preparation Time: 30 minutes

2 large cabbage leaves
1¾ cups (425 ml) **bonito dashi stock (page 13)**
½ teaspoon **salt**
1 teaspoon **vegetable oil**
2 **eggs**
Shichimi pepper blend, to taste, optional

1 Cut the cabbage leaves into bite-sized pieces.

2 Combine the cabbage and dashi in a pot over medium heat. Cover and bring to a boil, then reduce heat to low and simmer for 10 minutes. Season with the salt.

3 Heat the oil in a skillet over medium heat. Add the eggs and cook sunny-side up. Ladle the soup into two bowls. Top each serving with an egg and sprinkle with shichimi pepper blend if desired.

Flavor intensifiers

The umami from the broth and the aromatic shichimi pepper blend amplify the richness of the egg yolk.

Bonito dashi stock   Shichimi pepper blend

117kcal | Good for digestion | Detoxing

Enjoying Seasonal
Vegetables in Your Soups

Though many vegetables are available year-round, there is always a time of year when particular varieties are at their best. Of course, this varies, depending on the region and the vegetables. Freshly harvested produce in peak season is refreshingly crisp and packed with flavor. These vegetables make the best dashi stock, with rich umami.

These days, most grocery stores are able to carry produce year-round, thanks to crops grown in greenhouses and advances in storage technology. Unfortunately, the flavor of these vegetables cannot compare to that of vegetables harvested at their peak.

Seasonal crops also have a higher nutritional content than those harvested in the off-season. Needless to say, the extra vitamins and minerals are beneficial to your health—all the more reason to find ways to incorporate the season's bounty into the cooking you do at home.

Buying in large quantities brings costs down, so it may be wise to buy extra during the harvest season and freeze some for later.

SPRING VEGETABLES

Most vegetables harvested in the spring are succulent, with a clean taste and a tender texture. Foraged vegetables with distinctive bitterness, such as fern shoots and butterbur, become available in this season, as do aromatics like mitsuba (wild Japanese parsley). Using only salt for the seasoning brings out the crisp flavor of the spring vegetables.

Parsley

Celery

Carrot

If you want to incorporate more vegetables into your daily meals, soups are your best bet. It is hard to eat a lot of vegetables when they're raw. Simmered dishes often contain large amounts of sugar and oil, especially when purchased ready-made or ordered at a restaurant. Steamed vegetables tend to be low in calories, as the seasoning is minimal; however, the accompanying sauces and dressings may be loaded with salt and fat. Soups, however, made with umami-packed broth, don't need a lot of rich toppings to make them taste delicious.

SUMMER VEGETABLES

Warmer months yield bountiful, vitamin-rich harvests of vibrantly colored and flavorful produce. Vegetables in the gourd family, such as cucumbers and bitter gourds, are especially good to eat when the temperature soars, as they have cooling and fatigue-fighting properties. Spices and sour elements can also be used to great effect in the summer.

Kabocha squash

Tomatoes

Bitter gourd

Hen-of-the-woods mushrooms

Japanese sweet potato

Burdock

FALL VEGETABLES

This is the season when mushrooms and potatoes are at their most flavorful. Since fall is the peak harvest season, it brings an abundance of produce. Vegetables become rich in umami, with concentrated flavors. Use soy sauce and miso to complement the robust flavors.

Turnip

WINTER VEGETABLES

Vegetables grown in the colder months have a defense mechanism that makes them sweeter, more nutritious and more flavorful. The increased vitamin C content helps prevent and treat common colds. Slow-simmered soups that warm you up from the inside are perfect for this season.

Chrysanthemum greens

Cauliflower

Serves: 2
Preparation Time: 20 minutes

2 slender Asian eggplants
1 bell pepper
1 tomato
¼-inch (6 mm) piece ginger
2 teaspoons olive oil
1 3/4 cups (425 ml) bonito dashi stock
(page 13)
1 teaspoon soy sauce
1 teaspoon rice vinegar
2 green shiso or basil leaves

1 Remove the eggplant stems and peel the skin. Cut into thick rounds. Chop the bell pepper and tomato into triangular chunks. Mince the ginger.

2 Heat the oil in a pot over medium heat and sauté the ginger until fragrant. Add the eggplants and bell pepper and cook for a few minutes. Stir in the dashi and tomato, cover and bring to a boil. Reduce heat and simmer for 10 minutes.

3 Season with the soy sauce and vinegar. Garnish with chopped shiso to serve.

Serves: 2
Preparation Time: 20 minutes

2 new potatoes
2 cabbage leaves
10 sugar snap peas
2 cups (500 ml) bonito dashi stock (page 13)
1 tablespoon sake
½ teaspoon salt
Black pepper, to taste

1 Cut the potatoes into quarters and soak in water. Chop the cabbage into thick strips. Top and tail the sugar peas and split the pods in half lengthwise.

2 Combine the dashi, sake, drained potatoes and cabbage in a pot over medium heat. Cover and bring to a boil, then reduce heat to low and simmer for 10 minutes.

3 Add the sugar snap peas and cook for 5 more minutes. Season with the salt and pepper.

Summer Vegetable Soup

Combining a variety of brightly colored vegetables, this soup is light and refreshing. The rice vinegar and fresh herbs add piquancy.

80kcal	Good for digestion	Nourishes the skin	Anti-aging

122kcal	Good for digestion	Nourishes the skin	Detoxing

Spring Vegetable Soup

The seasoning is kept simple in this soup—just dashi stock, salt and pepper—to accentuate the freshness of spring vegetables.

Serves: 2
Preparation Time: 25 minutes

3-inch (7.5 cm) piece daikon
⅓ lotus root (or ½ small can water chestnuts)
½ cup (15 g) spinach
1 red chili pepper
½ sheet deep-fried tofu skin
2 cups (500 ml) bonito dashi stock (p. 13)
2 teaspoons mirin
2 teaspoons soy sauce

1 Cut the daikon and lotus root into thick quarter-moons. Soak the lotus root in water. Cut the spinach into 1-inch (2.5 cm) pieces. Halve the red chili pepper diagonally. Place the deep-fried tofu in a sieve and pour boiling water over to remove excess oil. Halve crosswise and then cut into strips.

2 Combine dashi, daikon and drained lotus root in a pot over medium heat. Cover, bring to a boil, then reduce heat and simmer for 15 minutes.

3 Add the red chili pepper, tofu, mirin and soy sauce. Bring to a gentle boil, add the spinach and cook for a few minutes more.

Serves: 2
Preparation Time: 25 minutes

2 taro roots, peeled and cut into chunks
1½ oz (40 g) hen-of-the-woods mushrooms
¼ onion
2 teaspoons butter
½ medium carrot, sliced into half moons
2 cups (500 ml) bonito dashi stock (p.13)
1 tablespoon miso
¼ cup (30 g) shredded cheddar or Colby cheese

1 Sprinkle the taro with salt and massage to remove the slippery coating, then rinse. Remove the base of the mushrooms. Tear the mushrooms into small segments. Slice the onion thinly.

2 Melt the butter in a pot over medium heat. Add the taro, carrot and onion. Stir in the dashi, cover and bring to a boil. Reduce heat to low. Simmer for 10 minutes.

3 Add the mushrooms and cook for 5 more minutes. Thin the miso with some of the broth from the pot, then stir into the soup. Add the cheese just before serving.

Winter Vegetable Soup

Using chili pepper in the colder season helps to warm the body from the inside.

90 kcal	Good for digestion	Wards off lifestyle diseases	Prevents lifestyle diseases	Detoxing

157 kcal	Good for digestion	Wards off lifestyle diseases

Fall Vegetable Soup

Using root vegetables and mushrooms at their flavorful height, this soup derives additional richness from miso, butter and cheese.

Tofu Potage

Packed with umami from the scallops, this soup is quite filling because of the mashed tofu.

Serves: 2
Preparation Time: 10 minutes

Piece silken tofu, about 6 oz (175 g)
2 oz (50 g) canned scallops, with liquid
¾ cup (185 ml) bonito dashi stock (page 13)
1 teaspoon potato or cornstarch
2 teaspoons water
½ cup (125 ml) soy milk
⅓ teaspoon salt
Aonori or dulse flakes, for garnish

1 Mash the tofu well.

2 Bring the dashi and canned scallops with liquid to a boil in a pot over medium heat. Add the mashed tofu. Mix the potato starch with the water and stir in.

3 Add the soy milk and return to a gentle boil. Season with the salt. Sprinkle with the aonori to serve.

Burdock and Taro Potage

Simmered burdock and taro roots make for a velvety and satisfyingly thick soup.

Serves: 2
Preparation Time: 30 minutes

8-inch (20 cm) piece burdock, or carrot
¼ baby leek (white and light green parts only)
1 taro root
½ tablespoon butter
1¼ cups (300 ml) dashi stock
1 tablespoon sake
½ cup (125 ml) milk
1 teaspoon soy sauce
Large pinch salt
Black pepper, to taste

1 Thinly slice the burdock and leek crosswise. Soak the burdock in water. Peel the taro root and cut into bite-sized pieces. Sprinkle with salt, massage to remove the slippery coating and rinse with water.

2 Melt the butter in a pot over medium heat and sauté the leek, drained burdock and taro root. Add the dashi and sake, cover and bring to a boil. Reduce heat to low and simmer for 20 minutes or until the burdock is soft.

3 Mash the vegetables, leaving some texture. Add the milk and bring to a gentle boil. Season with the soy sauce, salt and pepper.

Tofu Potage

93 kcal

Wards off lifestyle diseases

Anti-aging

Chunky Turnip Soup

The flavorful dashi melds beautifully with the mashed baby turnips. The white color is preserved nicely by keeping the seasoning minimal.

Serves: 2
Preparation Time: 30 minutes

4 baby turnips
1⅓ cups (425 ml) bonito dashi stock (page 13)
2 teaspoons sake
⅓ teaspoon salt
Black pepper, to taste
2 to 3 drops soy sauce
Zest of yuzu citrus or Meyer lemon

1 Peel the turnips and cut them into bite-sized pieces.

2 Combine the turnips, dashi and sake in a pot over medium heat. Cover and bring to a boil, then lower the heat and simmer for 20 minutes.

3 Mash the turnips, leaving some texture. Season with the salt, pepper and soy sauce. Garnish with a sliver of yuzu zest before serving.

Chunky Turnip Soup

34kcal

Good for digestion	Detoxing

Burdock and Taro Potage

112kcal

Good for digestion	Wards off lifestyle diseases

Easy Potages

In Japan, there is a type of soup called *surinagashi*, which means "ground and poured." Quite similar to a potage, this thick soup is prepared by cooking ingredients in dashi until soft and then mashing them. Here are some full-bodied soups that use the same technique.

Quick Soups

Umami-rich ingredients make delicious dashi stock when boiling water is poured over them. Add a little bit of seasoning, slightly crunchy vegetables and aromatics and you'll be able to enjoy a low-calorie soup that's ready in no time.

Umami-rich ingredients

Add hot water to enjoy a soup instantly!

Other ingredients

Boiling water

Done!

Instant soup

Quick Soup with Mizuna Greens

The savory shio kombu produces a nicely flavored broth. Mizuna adds a refreshing texture. Serves 2.

3 kcal

2 teaspoons shio kombu

+

2 to 3 stalks mizuna or arugula

+

1¼ cups (300 ml) boiling water

||

Cut the mizuna into 1-inch (2.5 cm) pieces. Divide the ingredients between 2 bowls and pour the boiling water over all.

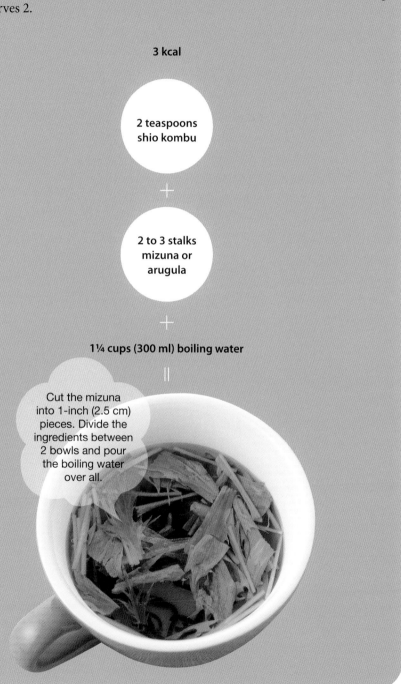

Ginger Soup with Bonito Flakes

Glutamates, the flavor enhancer in the bonito flakes, play the starring role in this soup. Serves 2.

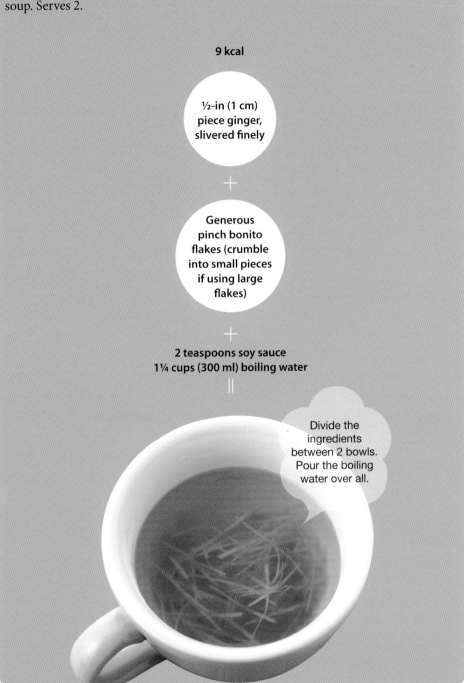

9 kcal

½-in (1 cm) piece ginger, slivered finely

+

Generous pinch bonito flakes (crumble into small pieces if using large flakes)

+

2 teaspoons soy sauce
1¼ cups (300 ml) boiling water

||

Divide the ingredients between 2 bowls. Pour the boiling water over all.

Kombu and Lettuce Soup

Tororo kombu adds umami and body to the soup. Serves 2.

8 kcal

Pinch tororo kombu

+

1 leaf lettuce, torn into pieces

+

**2 teaspoons soy sauce
1¼ cups (300 ml) boiling water**

=

Divide the lettuce and soy sauce between 2 bowls. Pour the boiling water over and add the tororo kombu.

Savory Ginger Soup with Umeboshi

Umeboshi and myoga ginger make a refreshing combination. Serves 2.

4 kcal

2 umeboshi salt-pickled plums

Small pinch bonito flakes (crumble into small pieces if necessary)

+

2 pieces myoga ginger bud, thinly sliced

+

1¼ cups (300 ml) boiling water

=

Break apart the umeboshi and divide between 2 bowls along with the thinly sliced myoga and bonito flakes. Pour the boiling water over all.

Miso Soup with Dried Shrimp and Green Onion

The umami of the sakura shrimp softens the sharpness of the green onion. Serves 2.

22 kcal

1 tablespoon sakura shrimp

+

1 fat green onion

+

2 teaspoons miso
1¼ cups (300 ml) boiling water

‖

Slice the green onion thinly and divide between 2 bowls along with the miso and sakura shrimp. Pour the boiling water over all and stir to dissolve the miso.

Sesame and Wakame Soup

The richness and aroma of sesame seeds add body to the broth. Serves 2.

15 kcal

1 teaspoon ground sesame seeds

+

6 sprigs mitsuba or flat-leaf parsley

½ teaspoon dried cut wakame

+

1 teaspoon kombu powder
1¼ cups (300 ml) boiling water

‖

Cut the mitsuba sprigs into 1-inch (2.5 cm) lengths and divide them between 2 bowls along with the kombu powder and ground sesame seeds. Pour the boiling water over all.

Mini Hotpot Soups

Balance Flavor and Nutrition with Mini Hotpot Soups

Slow-simmered soups are especially wonderful when prepared in small *donabe* (earthenware casseroles), ceramic cookware or Dutch ovens that can go directly from stovetop to table when ready. Cleanup is a breeze since the pots double as serving ware. Combine seafood, meat and vegetables for the best balance of flavor and nutrition.

Japanese Bouillabaisse

The classic French seafood stew is given a Japanese makeover by using bonito dashi stock as the base and adding soy sauce and sake. In addition to the shrimp, the vegetables and saffron bring umami to the dish.

Serves: 2
Preparation Time: 25 minutes

8 raw shrimp, peeled and deveined
Salt and pepper, to taste
¼ vacuum-packed precooked bamboo shoot, or 2½ oz (70 g)
    canned bamboo shoots
1 tomato
¼ clove garlic
½ baby leek or 1 fat green onion
2 teaspoons olive oil
1¾ cups (425 ml) bonito dashi stock (page 13)
2 pinches saffron threads
1 tablespoon sake
2 teaspoons soy sauce

1 Season the shrimp with salt and pepper. Cut the bamboo shoot into half-moons and the tomato into chunks. Mince the garlic; cut the leek or green onion into 1-inch (2.5 cm) pieces.

2 Heat the olive oil and garlic in a pot over low heat until fragrant. Turn up the heat and add the leek or green onion, bamboo shoot and tomato. Sauté for a minute or two.

3 Add the shrimp, dashi, saffron threads and sake and bring to a boil. Lower the heat and simmer for 7 to 8 minutes. Season with the soy sauce and additional black pepper.

141 kcal | Nourishes the skin | Prevents lifestyle diseases | Anti-aging

Health benefits

Tomato: Acts as an antioxidant, protects cell membranes
Saffron: Improves blood circulation, has a diuretic effect
Olive oil: Lowers cholesterol

Tomato   Saffron   Olive oil

Japanese Pot-au-feu

Seasoning is kept mild to bring out the flavor of the bonito dashi stock. The added knots of kombu amplify the umami factor. The sausages also impart depth to the broth.

Serves: 2
Preparation Time: 40 minutes

4 cocktail sausages
¼ head small cabbage
1 baby leek or 2 fat green onions
4-inch (10 cm) length daikon
½ carrot
1 piece kombu, about 7 x 2 inches (18 x 5 cm), soaked in water until pliable
2½ cups (625 ml) bonito dashi stock (page 13)
1 tablespoon sake
1 teaspoon soy sauce
½ teaspoon salt

1 Make shallow diagonal cuts on the surface of each sausage. Cut the cabbage into two wedges. Slice the leek or green onions into 1½-inch (4 cm) pieces. Cut the daikon and carrot into large chunks. Cut the rehydrated kombu in half lengthwise and tie each piece into a knot.

2 Combine the dashi, sake, cabbage, leek or green onions, daikon, carrot, and kombu knots in a pot over medium heat. Cover and bring to a boil, then lower heat and simmer for 20 minutes.

3 Add the cocktail sausages and cook for 4 to 5 minutes. Season with the soy sauce and salt.

191 kcal

| Good for digestion | Nourishes the skin | Wards off lifestyle diseases |

Health benefits

Carrot: Antioxidant effect, protects the cell membranes and skin
Kombu: Lowers blood pressure and cholesterol

Carrot   Kombu

Curried Tomato Soup with Pork Meatballs

Curry tends to be high in calories, but this vegetable-loaded soup is perfect for when you want to enjoy exotic flavors without a heavy meal. The pork and tomatoes add another layer of umami.

Serves: 2
Preparation Time: 30 minutes

5 oz (150 g) ground pork
1 teaspoon sake
2 teaspoons soy sauce, divided
½ teaspoon toasted sesame oil
Pinch black pepper
Large handful spinach
1¾ cups (425 ml) water
½ cup (100 g) cubed and peeled butternut or kabocha squash (if using kabocha, no need to peel)
½ cup (100 g) canned diced tomatoes, with liquid
½ teaspoon curry powder
Salt and pepper, to taste

1 Combine the pork, sake, 1 teaspoon of the soy sauce, sesame oil and black pepper in a bowl. Knead by hand until the mixture forms a thick paste. Shape the paste into small balls. Cut the spinach into 1-inch (2.5 cm) pieces.

2 Bring the water and squash to a boil in a covered pot over medium heat. Add the meatballs to the boiling water.

3 Stir in the tomatoes, curry powder, salt and pepper. Cover and return to the boil, then reduce heat to low and simmer for 15 minutes. Add the spinach and the remaining 1 teaspoon soy sauce. Cook for a few more minutes.

85 kcal

Good for digestion	Nourishes the skin	Wards off lifestyle diseases	Anti-aging

Health benefits

Squash: High in vitamins, minerals and antioxidants, lowering risk of disease. Curry powder: Boosts the metabolism and combats fatigue.

Kabocha squash

Curry powder

156kcal

Nourishes the skin | Prevents lifestyle diseases | Anti-aging

Salmon Meatball Soup

Tofu is added to the salmon meatballs to increase bulk while cutting down on the calories. This satisfying soup contains multiple sources of umami, including the kombu stock, shiitake mushrooms and salmon.

Serves: 2
Preparation Time: 30 minutes

1 salmon steak, about 4 oz (100 g) skin and bones removed
1 piece tofu, about 4 oz (100 g), drained and pressed
1 teaspoon sake
Dash each salt and pepper
2 tablespoons minced baby leek or green onions
6 oz (175 g) spinach
2 shiitake mushrooms, fresh or reconstituted, stems discarded
2-inch (5 cm) piece kombu
1¾ cups (425 ml) water
1 tablespoon sake
1 teaspoon soy sauce
¼ teaspoon salt

1 To make the salmon meatballs, finely chop the salmon and place in a bowl. Add the tofu, sake and salt and pepper. Knead by hand until the mixture becomes a thick paste. Mix in the minced leek or green onions and shape into bite-sized balls.

2 Cut the spinach into 1½-inch (4 cm) pieces. Halve the shiitake mushroom caps.

3 Wipe the kombu with a damp cloth. Bring the water and kombu to a simmer in a pot over medium heat. Remove the kombu just before the pot comes to a boil. Add the sake, meatballs and shiitake mushrooms. Let the pot come to a boil, then lower the heat and simmer for 10 minutes. Season with the soy sauce and salt. Add the spinach and cook for another minute or two.

Health benefits

Salmon: Improves blood circulation, activates the brain cells, strengthens the bones
Shiitake mushrooms: Lower cholesterol, help prevent high blood pressure and hardening of the arteries

Salmon   Shiitake
            mushrooms

Mountain Yam Soup

This soup showcases the textural contrast between the ingredients. The slippery texture of mountain yam and nameko mushrooms are attributed to mucin, a substance known to support the stomach, liver and kidneys.

Serves: 2
Preparation Time: 20 minutes

4-inch (10 cm) piece mountain yam
2 green onions (scallions) or 1 bunch chives
1¾ cups (425 ml) bonito dashi stock (page 13)
2 oz (50 g) nameko mushrooms, rinsed, or other mushrooms
1 teaspoon soy sauce
1 teaspoon mirin
⅓ teaspoon salt

1 Peel and grate the mountain yam using the finest side of a box grater. Thinly slice the green onions on the diagonal.

2 Bring the dashi to a boil in a pot over medium heat. Add the grated mountain yam, stirring in a quarter of the amount at a time. Simmer for 4 to 5 minutes.

3 Add the nameko mushrooms and bring to a gentle boil. Season with the soy sauce, mirin and salt. Garnish with the sliced green onions.

118kcal | **Good for digestion** | **Combats fatigue**

Health benefits

Mountain yam: Protects the stomach lining, promotes digestion, boosts stamina
Nameko mushrooms: Regulate the intestinal system

Mountain yam

Nameko mushrooms

Main Dish Soups

Hearty and Substantial
Main Dish Soups

Adding carbohydrates like rice, noodles or potatoes to a soup
makes a meal in itself that is really satisfying. The high fluid
content of soup means that you end up eating fewer calories
and still feel full. The main-dish soup recipes in this section
are a great choice for people trying to lose weight.

The Beauty of Slow-simmered Soups

Slow-simmered soups contain a delicious savor that eases tension and gives comfort to body and soul.

One of the great things about most of the soups in this book is that they can be prepared in a short amount of time. But once in a while it's nice to take some time to make a stew-like soup. Having a soup simmering on the stove imparts the same sort of relaxation as watching logs flicker quietly in the fireplace. The smell that fills the kitchen, the subdued murmuring sound of the pot simmering away and the way the ingredients start to fall apart . . . each of these elements helps melt away stress and dispels, at least for a little while, the busy reality of life.

Whether to make a big batch or a small pot just for yourself is up to you. These slow-simmered soups are warming and satisfying, with a flavor that will be even better the next day.

Some of these soups may take a little longer to make, but the luxurious and gratifying results make the time spent worthwhile.

Umami from each ingredient permeates the soup, so if you have leftover broth, try adding cooked rice, pasta or noodles to make a standalone light meal.

Japanese Onion Soup with Mochi Rice Cakes

The French classic is reinvented with a Japanese twist. Using dashi stock and soy sauce simplifies preparation, as the flavor is already there even if you don't have time to caramelize the onion. Mochi with cheese melted on top makes this soup very filling.

Serves: 2
Preparation Time: 30 minutes

1 medium onion
1 tablespoon butter
1¾ cups (425 ml) bonito dashi stock (page 13)
1 tablespoon sake
1 teaspoon soy sauce
Salt and pepper, to taste
2 pieces mochi
2 tablespoons shredded mild cheese
Cracked black pepper, for garnish

1 Slice the onion into thin half-moons. Melt the butter in a pot over medium heat and sauté the onion until golden brown. Add the dashi and sake, cover and bring to a boil. Simmer for 10 minutes over low heat and season with the soy sauce, salt and pepper.

2 Cut each piece of mochi in half and sprinkle cheese on top. Place on a baking sheet lined with greased aluminum foil and cook in an oven preheated to 400°F (200°C) for 15 minutes or until the mochi is puffed and cheese is melted.

3 Ladle the soup into bowls. Top with the mochi pieces and cracked black pepper to serve.

239kcal · Wards off lifestyle diseases

Hearty and filling ingredients

Grilled mochi has a delicious toasted flavor. Topped with melted cheese, it adds substance and richness to the soup.

Mochi   Cheese

Chicken Soup on Rice

The traditional Japanese dish called *ochazuke*, prepared by pouring green tea or dashi stock over cooked rice, makes a quick, filling meal. Here, Japanese aromatics are used to create a light and soothing soup that is then served on top of rice. You can also cook the rice together with everything else to make a porridge-like savory soup.

Serves: 2
Preparation Time :15 minutes

4 oz (100 g) boneless, skinless chicken breast or tenders
Salt for sprinkling, plus ⅓ teaspoon for seasoning
3 tablespoons shiso pickles (kimchi or sauerkraut will also work)
4 sprigs mitsuba or flat-leaf parsley
1¾ cups (425 ml) bonito dashi stock (page 13)
1 tablespoon sake
2 bowls warm rice

1 Slice the chicken at an angle and sprinkle with salt. Chop the pickles. Cut the mitsuba into 1-inch (2.5 cm) pieces.

2 Bring the dashi to a boil in a pot over medium heat. Add the sake and the chicken from step 1. After the pot returns to the boil, simmer for 4 to 5 minutes and season with the ⅓ teaspoon salt.

3 Pour the chicken/dashi mixture from step 2 over the warm rice in each bowl. Top with the chopped shiso pickles and mitsuba.

Hearty and filling ingredients

Chicken breast meat is high in protein and low in calories. Combined with the rice, this makes a satisfying meal in itself.

Rice | Chicken breast or tenders

Minestrone with Soba Noodles

Incorporating Japanese vegetables in this Italian soup together with tomato and olive oil creates a marriage of umami from two different cultures. Using soba noodles in place of pasta is yet another tasty twist.

Serves: 2
Preparation Time: 30 minutes

¼ baby leek or ½ fat green onion
1 napa cabbage leaf
⅓ medium carrot
1 tomato
1 taro root
Salt for sprinkling, plus ⅓ teaspoon
4 oz (100 g) uncooked soba noodles
2 teaspoons olive oil
2½ cups (625 ml) bonito dashi stock
  (page 13)
1 tablespoon soy sauce
½ tablespoon mirin

1 Cut the leek or onions and napa cabbage into 1-inch (2.5 cm) pieces. Dice the carrot and tomato. Peel and dice the taro root. Sprinkle salt over the taro root, massage by hand and rinse with water to remove the slippery coating. Cook the soba noodles according to the directions on the package, drain and set aside.

2 Heat the olive oil in a pot over medium heat and sauté the vegetables from step 1 until coated with oil. Add the dashi, cover and bring to a boil. Reduce heat to low and simmer for 15 to 20 minutes.

3 Season with the soy sauce, mirin and salt. Cut the cooked soba noodles roughly in half and add to the pot. Let the soup return to a gentle boil.

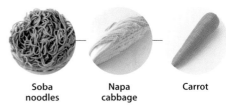

Soba noodles — Napa cabbage — Carrot

Hearty and filling ingredients

Because the soup is loaded with vegetables, you can get away with reducing the quantity of soba noodles if you want to cut down on carbs.

218kcal

| Good for digestion | Nourishes the skin | Wards off lifestyle diseases |

Tom Yum Soup

This popular soup from Thailand is given a Japanese twist by replacing fish sauce—which some people might find overpowering—with soy sauce. The flavors of sakura shrimp, bonito dashi stock and ginger are amplified in this vegetable-dense soup.

Serves: 2
Preparation Time: 30 minutes

2 king oyster mushrooms
½ baby leek or 1 fat green onion
4 shishito peppers (or ½ bell pepper)
¼-inch (6 mm) piece ginger
1 red chili pepper
4 oz (100 g) somen noodles, or angel hair pasta
2½ cups (625 ml) bonito dashi stock (page 13)
2 tablespoons sakura shrimp
1 tablespoon sake
¼ vacuum-packed precooked bamboo shoot, or 2½ oz (70 g) canned bamboo shoots, cut into wedges
½ teaspoon salt
½ teaspoon soy sauce
2 teaspoons rice vinegar
1 lemon slice, halved

1 Slice the king oyster mushrooms into thin rounds and cut the baby leek or green onions into bite-size pieces. Cut a slit along the length of each shishito pepper. Cut the ginger into thin matchsticks and thinly slice the red chili pepper into rings.

2 Cook the somen noodles according to the directions on the package.

3 Bring the dashi, sakura shrimp and sake to a boil in a pot over medium heat. Add the bamboo shoot, king oyster mushrooms, red chili pepper, ginger and leek or green onions and cook for a few minutes. Season with the salt, soy sauce and vinegar. Add the shishito peppers and the somen noodles from step 2. Allow to return to a boil. Top each serving with half a lemon slice.

229kcal

Good for digestion	Boosts metabolism	Nourishes the skin

Hearty and filling ingredients

The combination of smooth somen noodles and vegetables with contrasting textures makes every bite satisfying and delicious.

Somen noodles

King oyster mushrooms

Shrimp Wonton Soup

In this popular Chinese dish, shrimp wontons are simmered together with mushrooms in a kombu dashi stock seasoned with soy sauce. The texture of the shrimp in the wontons heightens the delectable experience.

Serves: 2
Preparation Time: 30 minutes

8 raw shrimp
1 teaspoon sake
½ teaspoon ginger juice
Dash each salt and pepper
2 tablespoons minced baby leek or
    green onions
10 wonton wrappers
½ bunch enoki mushrooms, or
    other mushrooms, trimmed
4 sprigs mitsuba, or flat-leaf parsley
2 cups (500 ml) kombu dashi stock
    (page 15)
½ teaspoon soy sauce
Large pinch salt

Hearty and filling ingredients

Adding enoki mushrooms makes the wonton soup extra substantial.

1 Peel, devein and finely chop the shrimp. Combine with the sake, ginger juice, salt and pepper and baby leek or onions and mix well. Put a spoonful of the filling in the center of a wonton wrapper, wet the edges with a finger dipped in water, then fold in half to form a triangle and press the edges to seal. Repeat the process with the remaining filling to make 10 wontons.

2 Cut the enoki mushrooms in half crosswise. Chop the mitsuba coarsely.

3 Bring the dashi to a boil in a pot over medium heat. Add the wontons and enoki mushrooms. Reduce heat and simmer for 4 to 5 minutes. Season with the soy sauce and salt, and finish with the mitsuba.

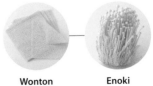

Wonton
wrappers

Enoki
mushrooms

Glass Noodle Soup with Squid and Broccoli

There are many varieties of Japanese instant noodles. Glass noodles are especially popular with people who are trying to lose weight. Preparing a soup from scratch gives you the option to add a good quantity of vegetables and reduce the sodium level, making the dish even healthier.

Serves: 2
Preparation Time: 30 minutes

2 oz (50 g) glass noodles (or thin rice noodles)
½ squid, about 2 oz (50 g)
¼ large head broccoli
¼-inch (6 mm) piece ginger
2 cups (500 ml) bonito dashi stock (page 13)
1 tablespoon sake
1 teaspoon soy sauce
⅓ teaspoon salt

1 Soak the glass noodles in boiling water until pliable. Skin the squid, score both sides of the flesh in a crosshatch pattern and cut into short strips. Cut the broccoli into small florets. Grate the ginger.

2 Bring the dashi to a boil in a pot over medium heat. Add the sake, broccoli and squid. Season with the soy sauce and salt.

3 Add the glass noodles and let the soup return to the boil. Garnish each serving with grated ginger.

150kcal Boosts metabolism Anti-aging Detoxing

Hearty and filling ingredients

The chewiness of the glass noodles and squid helps stimulate the satiety center in the brain, making you feel satisfied even if you don't eat a large amount.

Glass noodles

Squid

Grilled Rice-ball Soup with Crispy Pork

Grilled rice balls team up with crispy fried pork to release deep flavors. Grated daikon thickens the broth.

Serves: 2
Preparation Time: 30 minutes

3–4 thin slices pork belly, about 3½ oz (85 g)
Salt and pepper for sprinkling , plus ⅓ teaspoon salt for
  seasoning
12 snow peas
1¾ cups (320 g) cooked rice
1¾ cups (425 ml) dashi stock
3-inch (7.5 cm) piece daikon, grated and drained
1 teaspoon soy sauce

1 Cut the pork into 2-inch (5 cm) pieces and sprinkle with salt and pepper. Thinly slice the snow peas on the diagonal. Divide the cooked rice into 4 portions. Dampen your hands with water and firmly compress the rice into a flattened triangle or ball. Repeat with the rest of the rice.

2 Fry the pork in a skillet over high heat. Transfer the meat to a separate bowl and then grill the rice balls on both sides in the same skillet.

3 Bring the dashi to a boil in a pot. Season with the soy sauce and salt. Add the snow peas and grated daikon. Let the pot return to the boil. To serve, divide rice balls and pork between two bowls and pour the soup over them.

363kcal | Good for digestion | Detoxing

Hearty and filling ingredients

Searing the pork and rice balls imparts a grilled flavor to the soup.

Rice   Pork

Miso Soup with Salmon and Vegetables

This recipe transforms a traditional salmon hotpot from the northern part of Japan into a soup. Using nicely sized chunks of fish in the soup makes for a greater sense of well-being and satisfaction. The sake lees round out the flavor and also help promote circulation.

Serves: 2
Preparation Time: 30 minutes

1½ tablespoons sake lees
2 cups (500 ml) kombu dashi stock (page 15), divided
1 salmon steak, about 4 oz (100 g), bones removed
Salt and pepper for sprinkling
2 medium potatoes
½ medium carrot
1 cabbage leaf
2 teaspoons miso

1 Soak the sake lees in ¼ cup (65 ml) of the dashi to soften. Cut the salmon into bite-sized pieces and sprinkle with salt and pepper.

2 Cut the potatoes, carrot and cabbage into chunks. Soak the potatoes in water.

3 Combine the remaining dashi, drained potatoes and carrot in a pot over medium heat. Cover and bring to a boil, then reduce heat to low and simmer for 15 minutes. Add the salmon and cabbage and cook for 4 to 5 minutes more. Stir in the soaked sake lees and miso at the end.

250kcal

| Good for digestion | Nourishes the skin | Wards off lifestyle diseases |

Hearty and filling ingredients

There are no grains in this soup, but potatoes and chunks of salmon add heft and volume.

Potato   Carrot   Sake lees

260kcal | Nourishes the skin | Wards off lifestyle diseases

Cod and Vegetable Soup with Penne

Many pasta dishes are high in calories, but this light and tasty soup is not. The garnish of ground sesame seeds adds depth and richness, making for a really satisfying dish.

Serves: 2
Preparation Time: 30 minutes

¼ onion
½ zucchini
¼ red bell pepper
4 oz (100 g) cod
Salt and pepper, to taste
4 oz (100 g) penne pasta
2 teaspoons olive oil
Sliced garlic, to taste
2 cups (500 ml) kombu dashi stock (page 15)
1 tablespoon sake
2 teaspoons soy sauce
⅓ teaspoon salt
Black pepper, to taste
1 teaspoon ground sesame seeds
1 teaspoon grated Parmesan

1 Dice the onion small. Slice the zucchini into thick half-moons and cut the bell pepper into triangular chunks. Cut the cod into bite-sized pieces and sprinkle with salt and pepper. Cook the pasta in salted water according to the directions on the package. Drain and set aside.

2 Heat the olive oil in a pot over medium heat and sauté the garlic and onion. Add the zucchini and bell pepper and cook for a few more minutes. Stir in the dashi and the sake and bring the pot to a boil. Add the cod and allow to return to the boil. Cover, reduce heat to low and simmer for 10 minutes.

3 Add the pasta and season with the soy sauce, ⅓ teaspoon salt and additional pepper. Sprinkle the ground sesame seeds and grated Parmesan on top to serve.

Hearty and filling ingredients

The penne is filling and the chunks of cod are satisfying. Both add up to make a delicious soup that is relatively low in calories.

Penne   Cod

Pumpkin Soup with Mochi Dumplings

Use butternut or kabocha squash to give a rich, sweet flavor. With tender kernels of sweet corn and chewy mochi dumplings, this soup is a resplendent meal in itself.

Serves: 2
Preparation Time: 35 minutes

1 strip bacon
½ cup (80 g) glutinous rice flour (*mochiko*)
¼ cup (65 ml) water
1¼ cups (300 ml) dashi stock
1 cup (200 g) cubed and peeled butternut or kabocha squash (if using kabocha, no need to peel)
4 tablespoons canned sweet corn, drained
2 teaspoons miso
¾ cup (185 ml) milk
Black pepper, to taste

1 Quarter the bacon crosswise.

2 Bring a large pot of water to a boil. Meanwhile, combine the glutinous rice flour and water in a bowl and knead to make a soft dough. Tear off bite-sized pieces of the dough, shape each one into a ball and press the center of each ball with your thumb to make a flat disc. Cook the dumplings in the boiling water until they rise to the surface. Drain and set aside.

3 Bring the dashi and squash to a boil in a separate covered pot. Add the bacon and sweet corn, reduce heat to low and simmer for 15 to 20 minutes. Thin the miso with some of the broth from the pot, and then stir it in along with the milk and black pepper. Let the pot return to a gentle boil and add the mochi dumplings.

411 kcal | Good for digestion | Nourishes the skin | Anti-aging

Hearty and filling ingredients

Butternut or kabocha squash and mochi dumplings make a very satisfying soup. Milk enriches the soup and mellows out the flavor.

Mochiko   Kabocha squash

Milk

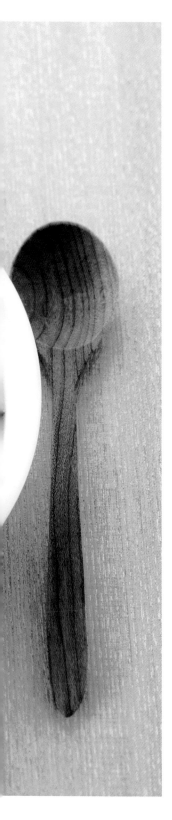

Barley Soup with Sweet Potato

The starchy texture of the sweet potato combines well with the chewy barley in this fiber- and vitamin-rich soup. The seasoning is kept simple to bring out the sweetness in the sweet potato and aroma of the greens.

Serves: 2
Preparation Time: 35 minutes

4 tablespoons pressed barley or pearl barley
1 sweet potato, about 5 oz (150 g)
1 stalk chrysanthemum greens, or handful mustard greens
2 cups (500 ml) bonito dashi stock (page 13)
½ teaspoon soy sauce
⅓ teaspoon salt
Black pepper, to taste

1 Rinse the pressed barley and soak in water for about 30 minutes to soften (soaking is not necessary if using pearl barley). Drain and set aside.

2 Slice the sweet potato into 1-inch (2.5 cm) thick rounds and then cut each slice into quarters. Cut the greens into 1-inch (2.5 cm) pieces.

3 Bring the dashi, drained barley and sweet potato to a boil in a covered pot over medium heat. Lower the heat and simmer for 20 minutes. Season with the soy sauce, salt and black pepper. Add the greens and cook for another minute or two.

180kcal | Good for digestion | Nourishes the skin

Hearty and filling ingredients

The two starring ingredients in this soup, sweet potato and pressed barley, are both rich in fiber. This soup will fill you up and stick to your ribs.

Pressed barley   Japanese sweet potato

Garnishes and Finishing Touches

In Japanese cuisine, the term *suikuchi* refers to the garnish added at the end of cooking to round out the dish. The same technique can be applied when making soups. Even just adding an aromatic ingredient as a finishing touch can spark up a soup.

If you have ever had a clear broth soup at a Japanese restaurant, you can visualize the concept of *suikuchi*. Merely giving dashi stock a salty flavor would be too one-dimensional. But if you added some chopped green onions, yuzu citrus zest or shichimi pepper, you can immediately taste the difference.

Adding an aromatic garnish at the end transforms a soup, giving the refined flavor that is highly esteemed in Japanese cuisine. Because the soups in this book were developed based on the principles of traditional Japanese cooking, aromatics play a very important role. They bring qualities like piquancy, spiciness, texture and umami, adding complexity and depth.

For soups with bold elements, add the zest or juice of yuzu, lemon or another citrus to balance out the flavors. Chopped shiso leaves or umeboshi salt-pickled plums would also work in well here, adding an assertive, refreshing aroma.

PIQUANCY

In addition to their tangy juice, citrus fruits are prized for their distinctive, refreshing fragrance. The brightly colored zest adds visual pleasure. The sour, salty kick of umeboshi salt-pickled plum also adds an assertive brightness to soup. Breaking it apart intensifies the flavor.

Citruses

Umeboshi
salt-pickled
plums

On the other hand, for mild-tasting soups, sprinkle on some sesame seeds, grated cheese, nuts or green onion to add richness. In addition to using these ingredients as garnishes, you can incorporate them during cooking to add complexity to the flavor and contrast to the textures.

If your soup turns out tasting a bit flat, sprinkling in some hot or peppery spices can help to bring the flavor together, turning a run-of-the-mill soup into something you'll savor till the very last bite.

When you are using mild ingredients with a subtle flavor, give your soup a little boost of umami by adding savory bonito flakes, sakura shrimp or shio kombu.

PUNGENCY

Shichimi pepper blend, Japanese chili powder and black pepper can be used to add pungency to dishes. In addition to providing intense heat, most have a nice aroma. It is best to have each person sprinkle these spices on their own bowl, as heat tolerance depends on the individual.

Shichimi pepper blend

Black pepper

TEXTURE

Aromatics are a great way to add texture, especially when the soup contains soft ingredients that contrast well with additions such as nutty sesame seeds, crisp green onions or crunchy nuts. These textural differences let the natural flavor of each ingredient shine.

Sesame seeds

Green onions

UMAMI

As long as it can be consumed without being heated through, any umami-rich ingredient can be added as a topping at the end. Bonito flakes and sakura shrimp are particularly useful, as they add aroma while enhancing flavors.

Sakura shrimp

Bonito flakes

Banish Hunger Pangs with Late-Night Soups

Eating late at night can contribute to weight gain. Although we all know that's a fact, sometimes it's hard to think straight when hunger strikes. Low-calorie soups make excellent late-night snacks because they are easily digestible and provide just the right amount of satiety. Of course, the fact that they are a snap to prepare and require minimal cleanup is a huge plus!

13kcal | Good for digestion | Prevents lifestyle diseases

Mushroom Soup

Low-calorie and fiber-rich mushrooms are front and center in this soup. The lime slices contain citric acid to help fight fatigue while adding refreshing acidity.

Serves: 2
Preparation Time: 15 minutes

3 shiitake mushrooms, fresh or
    reconstituted
Handful shimeji or other
    mushrooms, about 1½ oz (40 g)
4 sprigs of flat-leaf parsley
1¾ cups (425 ml) water
1 tablespoon sake
1 teaspoon soy sauce
⅓ teaspoon salt
2 lime slices

1 Discard the stems of the shiitake mushrooms and cut the caps into wedges. Cut off the base of the mushrooms and pull them apart into smaller clumps. Chop the parsley into 1-inch (2.5 cm) pieces.

2 Bring the water, sake, shiitake and mushrooms to a boil in a pot over medium heat. Reduce heat to low and simmer for 7 to 8 minutes.

3 Season with the soy sauce and salt, then add the parsley and cook for one minute. Serve with a slice of lime alongside.

Wakame Seaweed Soup with Bean Sprouts

The deep-fried tofu skin and the bean sprouts lend sweetness and extra umami to the broth. This soup has plenty of iodine-rich wakame to help boost the metabolism.

Serves: 2
Preparation Time: 20 minutes

¾ cup (70 g) soybean or mung bean sprouts
1 teaspoon dried cut wakame seaweed
½ sheet deep-fried tofu skin
1¾ cups (425 ml) bonito dashi stock (page 13)
1 teaspoon soy sauce
¼ teaspoon salt

1 Place the deep-fried tofu skin in a sieve and pour boiling water over it to remove excess oil. Squeeze briefly and cut into thin strips.

2 Bring the dashi to a boil over medium heat. Add the wakame, bean sprouts and deep-fried tofu.

3 Season with the soy sauce and salt.

63 kcal

Good for digestion

Prevents lifestyle diseases

35 kcal

| Good for digestion | Prevents lifestyle diseases |

Mountain Yam and Okra Soup

Vegetables with a gelatinous texture, like mountain yam, okra and nameko mushrooms, aid digestion and support the intestines while activating the cells in the body to defend against damage caused by oxidants.

Serves: 2
Preparation Time: 20 minutes

1½-inch (4 cm) piece mountain yam
2 okra pods
1½ oz (40 g) nameko mushrooms
1¾ cups (425 ml) dashi stock
1 teaspoon soy sauce
⅓ teaspoon salt

1 Peel the mountain yam and cut into matchsticks. Slice the okra into rings. Rinse the nameko mushrooms.

2 Bring the dashi to a boil over medium high heat. Add the mountain yam and cook until the pot returns to a boil.

3 Add the soy sauce, salt, okra and mushrooms and cook for another minute.

Carrot-ginger Soup

Carotene-rich with antioxidant properties, carrots make a great pairing with a generous dose of warming ginger that aids digestion.

Serves: 2
Preparation Time: 15 minutes

½ medium carrot
½-inch (1 cm) piece ginger
1¼ cups (300 ml) water
½ teaspoon kombu powder
Salt, to taste

1 Cut the carrot into thin matchsticks. Cut the ginger into fine slivers.

2 Bring the water, carrot and ginger to a boil in a covered pot over medium high heat. Reduce heat to low and simmer for 7 to 8 minutes.

3 Season with the kombu powder and salt.

13kcal

| Nourishes the skin | Anti-aging | Wards off lifestyle diseases |

Index of main ingredients

Photo credits

"Books to Span the East and West"

Tuttle Publishing was founded in 1832 in the small New England town of Rutland, Vermont [USA]. Our core values remain as strong today as they were then—to publish best-in-class books which bring people together one page at a time. In 1948, we established a publishing office in Japan—and Tuttle is now a leader in publishing English-language books about the arts, languages and cultures of Asia. The world has become a much smaller place today and Asia's economic and cultural influence has grown. Yet the need for meaningful dialogue and information about this diverse region has never been greater. Over the past seven decades, Tuttle has published thousands of books on subjects ranging from martial arts and paper crafts to language learning and literature—and our talented authors, illustrators, designers and photographers have won many prestigious awards. We welcome you to explore the wealth of information available on Asia at **www.tuttlepublishing.com**.

Published by Tuttle Publishing, an imprint of
Periplus Editions (HK) Ltd.

WA SOUP © keiko iwasaki 2011
English translation rights arranged with Nitto Shoin Honsha
Co., Ltd. through Japan UNI Agency, Inc., Tokyo

English translation by Yukiko Sato.
English translation © 2020 Periplus Editions (HK) Ltd.

24 23 22 21   10 9 8 7 6 5 4 3 2
Printed in Malaysia   2104VP

ISBN 978-4-8053-1589-7

TUTTLE PUBLISHING® is a registered
trademark of Tuttle Publishing, a division of
Periplus Editions (HK) Ltd.

www.tuttlepublishing.com

Distributed by

North America, Latin America & Europe
Tuttle Publishing
364 Innovation Drive, North Clarendon,
VT 05759-9436 U.S.A.
Tel: 1 (802) 773-8930
Fax: 1 (802) 773-6993
info@tuttlepublishing.com
www.tuttlepublishing.com

Japan
Tuttle Publishing
Yaekari Building 3rd Floor, 5-4-12 Osaki,
Shinagawa-ku
Tokyo 141-0032
Tel: (81) 3 5437-0171; Fax: (81) 3 5437-0755
sales@tuttle.co.jp; www.tuttle.co.jp

Asia Pacific
Berkeley Books Pte. Ltd.
3 Kallang Sector #04-01, Singapore 349278
Tel: (65) 6741 2178
Fax: (65) 6741 2179
inquiries@periplus.com.sg
www.tuttlepublishing.com